The Pain and Joy of Ministry

THE PAIN AND JOY
OF MINISTRY

Harold R. Fray, Jr.

A Pilgrim Press Book
Philadelphia

To Susan

    John

        David

            Catherine

                Helen

                    Paul

CONTENTS

The Pain and Joy of Ministry

INTRODUCTION

The years 1969 to 1971 will go down in the history of the American Protestant church as the period in which the major initiatives taken in "the struggle for justice and peace" were taken not by national church bodies but by local churches and regional judicatories. Prior to this time Protestant strategy in civil rights and in the witness for peace was developed largely by national church agencies, either denominationally or interdenominationally.

Certainly nationally developed plans and programs in the early and mid-sixties had their impact on local churches and state conferences. Voter registration drives in the deep South became the seedbed for a new kind of leadership in local churches across the country. Although the earliest protests against the Vietnam War were generated by denominational agencies responsible for social action and by groups like Clergy and Laymen Concerned About Vietnam, the tide of protest began to arise from local and regional church bodies after the Moratorium of November 1969.

Harold R. Fray, Jr., minister of Eliot Church, Newton, Massachusetts, chronicles in this book the changing of the tide and its implications for the life of the local church and especially for the role of the local minister.

One sees clearly in these pages an emerging new style of ministry. And yet it is not a book about the ordained ministry as such. It is a book about the life of the church—the church in a time of revolution striving to fulfill its dual role as obstetrician to a new age and pioneer of a new kind of community.

It is against this background that Harold Fray raises the question about the role of leadership in the church today. He does not deal with the question in abstract terms. He does it rather in narrative terms. If, as I believe, biblical theology is "recital," pastoral theology ought also to consist of the recital of the mighty acts of God through his church and its ministry. Of course it is always difficult to judge clearly the significance of the events in which one is himself a participant. But we find in the events set forth here (not all of them autobiographical) a

11

clear sense of the prophetic, critical, reconciling and humanizing call of the ministry.

These events whether they occurred in Newton, in the Massachusetts Conference, in Fremont, Nebraska are not closed chapters by any means. In each case they mark a new beginning—it is not too much to say, a breaking-in of God's kingdom. Because of the discontinuity with that which had gone before, it was only natural that conflict should arise. As a consequence we see the church struggling to find creative ways of dealing with conflict. The opportunities for open dialogue, the recognition of the need for pluralism, the consequent loss of membership and of support when hard decisions have to be made—all of this constitutes a new situation for the American church requiring deeply sensitive and highly skilled leadership.

It is not a new discovery that the local congregation comes alive when it deals with life and death issues. But it can deal with them more effectively when it has an enabler who sees those issues and interprets them in the light of the biblical tradition, and who in his own relationships within the congregation creates new levels of trust and collegiality.

"Nothing is real until it is local." The pain and joy of ministry are real and local in this book. But for one minister at least the joy far outweighs the pain.

Robert V. Moss, Jr., President
United Church of Christ

PREFACE

> Looking to Jesus the pioneer and perfecter of our faith, who for the joy that was set before him endured the cross.
> Hebrews 12:2

The church claims to have a word of "Good News" for all people under all circumstances. But that word is communicated through human beings who are able to relate the "Good News" to the changing circumstances of life. . . . "We are ambassadors for Christ, God making his appeal through us (2 Cor. 5:20)." The test for the church today is whether it can fulfill its vocation under radically changing conditions.

In his book *Future Shock*, Toffler asks the appropriate question: can the human organism adapt successfully to the incredible speed of change today, causing the human personality to experience profound anxiety and feelings of dislocation? He compares man's existence to eight hundred lifetimes of sixty years, stretched over a period of fifty thousand years, and lifts up what it means to live in the present moment:

> Of these eight hundred, fully six hundred and fifty were spent in caves. Only during the past seventy lifetimes has it been possible to communicate effectively from one lifetime to another—as writing made it possible to do. Only during the past six lifetimes have masses of men ever seen a printed word. Only during the past four has it been possible to measure time with any precision. Only in the past two has anyone anywhere used an electric motor. And the overwhelming majority of all the material goods we use in daily life today have been developed within the present, the eight-hundredth lifetime.[1]

Traditionally the Christian church has described the life of faith as a pilgrimage, but the human propensity has been to *settle down,* and find meaning and security in those forms and formulas which are familiar and time-tested. *That possibility is now gone.* That is the shocking fact under which the modern world is reeling as we see our institutions collapse, our traditions rooted up, and a new society taking shape over which we seem

---

[1] Alvin Toffler, *Future Shock* (New York: Random House, 1970), p. 13. Copyright 1970 Random House, Inc.

to have no control and in which we feel as strangers and aliens. Does the church have a word of "Good News" for the new world emerging? By definition, the answer is yes—for the new world is God's world, as much as the old. The question is whether the institutional church can make the transition.

This book is the "raw data" of the church struggling for its vocational identity. The stories of faith and fear, pain and joy are drawn from one denomination—the United Church of Christ —but the reader will find their counterparts in all branches of Christendom. The issues penetrate every segment of the Church of Christ: equipping clergy and laity to cope adequately and creatively with controversy, conflict and change; the development of leadership rooted in the capacity for openness, risk and vulnerability; the creation of organizational skills enabling the church to move from bureaucracy to adhocracy; and the formation of support structures that will make research, development, and experimentation a possibility at every level of the church's life.

Biblical faith is storytelling—the drama of man's relationship to God and his fellowman. The stories of these chapters are drawn from the local church, state conferences and national instrumentalities. They reveal success and failure, and the church's continuing effort to discover and express the "Good News" of the gospel of Christ in a changing world.

I have profound gratitude for those with whom I have shared the pilgrimage of faith, especially my wife, the staff and members of the United Parish of Newton (comprised of First, Second and Eliot Churches of Newton), and those with whom I have worked and struggled—cried and rejoiced—in the United Church of Christ.

I want to express particular appreciation to Dr. Robert V. Moss, Jr., President of the United Church of Christ, for his willingness to write an introduction to these stories of the church at work; to Mrs. Joan Whitaker, secretary of the Eliot Church, for her patient labors in typing and retyping this manuscript; and to those persons who have given me permission to quote from their personal communications and copyrighted materials.

Chapter 1
OUT OF THE DEPTHS

Out of the depths I cry to thee, O Lord.
  Lord, hear my voice.
Let thy ears be attentive
  to the voice of my supplications.
Psalm 130:1-2

"I hurt . . . I hurt . . . I HURT . . . I HURT." Those words were a slow, carefully modulated, gutteral sound at first, but as the muscles tightened along his neck, and his taut arms began to move, the pained expression grew in crescendo; until finally they ripped the air in an agonizing scream. "I HURT, I HURT, I HURT."

Perspiration stood out on his brow, and the sweat began to pour from the pores of those of us gathered about him. A clammy hand reached out to offer support to his wife, who had shared the hurt of her minister husband, and now experienced again the renewal of their pain, as he expressed for them and their children, the trauma of being *forced* to leave his church.

The issue was familiar. As a minister of the gospel of Jesus Christ, the demand for brotherhood and justice among whites and blacks was clear to him. But the specific implementation of that demand was strongly resisted in the church he served. A white neighborhood was becoming black and human emotions outstripped Christian love. As minister, perhaps he did not handle the situation perfectly—who does—but those of us gathered about him at that moment, when the visceral agony of his soul poured forth, could not doubt the price he and his family had paid for the stand he had taken. The friction and the tension proved too much to continue his ministry and he left his church deeply wounded in spirit.

Would he rise again? Or was he crushed by a load too heavy to bear? One could not be sure. His physical posture revealed his trial of soul. Without embarrassment, tears streamed down the faces of those of us who heard his cries, and understood, because we shared his vocation of Christian ministry. His shrieks of pain found their echoes in the depths of our own souls. We, too, had discovered that the Christian ministry is a painful vocation. Without that common experience we would not have been together at all.

We were a group of 20 men and women—ministers and ministers' wives, all members of the United Church of Christ—gathered for a 24-hour marathon that would launch us into ten days of intense painful and ecstatic relationships together. On the Laforet Conference grounds, Colorado Springs, Colorado, three other groups were gathered sharing comparable experiences. Our purpose was to probe the question, what is required today to equip men and women for Christian ministry?

It has long been clear that there is deep, profound trouble within the ranks of the clergy and their families. Only the most naive, or those unwilling to face the harsh truth, could miss the reality of malaise among the clergy. It has been a subject in the popular press and substantiated by the increasing number of seminary graduates who prefer to channel their ministries into fields other than the local parish. But the ranks of the alienated have not been confined to the young, as large numbers of older clergymen of all denominations, who have served local churches for years, join the drop-outs. Now the facts are substantiated by the publication of a recent study on why clergymen are making their exodus out of the local church.[1]

Those who gathered at Laforet in the summer of 1969 were not new to the parish ministry. We were the veterans—the ones who had experienced the rich rewards of Christian ministry—but who also knew the growing pain, frustration and sense of inadequacy that were increasingly a part of our labors in the local church. We knew through hard and harsh experience, that the local church was caught in the midst of profound and fundamental changes. We were the ones in the middle. Our seminary training and continued exposure to the best in theological and biblical studies on the role of the local church[2] made us acutely aware of the need for changes and new emphases if the church was to be relevant in a society undergoing a radical and irreversible reorientation and remain a servant institution in the service

---

[1] Gerald J. Jud, Edgar W. Mills, Jr., Genevieve Walters Burch, *Ex-Pastors: Why Men Leave the Parish Ministry* (Philadelphia: Pilgrim Press, 1970).

[2] See *The Church for Others, Two Reports on the Missionary Structure of the Congregation* (Geneva: World Council of Churches, 1967).

of man. A layman, whose training is in the field of biochemistry, summed up the challenge:

> The mark of a living organism is its capacity to change and adapt.

Then he added,

> Is the church alive?

Some of us have wondered.

We have also experienced the profound frustration and deep alienation of life-long church members, who have given of their substance and their service to their church for years, and now find themselves in utter confusion, with feelings of bitter resentment, as their minister seeks to move the church toward new styles of leadership and new areas of service. Their responses are both understandable and human. There is resistance. There is misunderstanding. There is resentment. There is hurt. They cannot understand the constant press toward change. They feel that their forms of ministry and service—to which they have been accustomed over a lifetime—are being neglected and negated. Inevitably it communicates a feeling of personal rejection, which no amount of reassurance can placate. As one woman said, "I feel that my church is being taken away from me. Don't you realize that I have nothing left?"

The minister is caught in the crunch. His training and study prompt him to seek to provide the kind of leadership that will enable the local church to be responsive to human needs. The mandate is clear: the Church of Jesus Christ is a servant community that exists for the sake of the world.[3] To press for anything less denies the calling of Christian vocation and the minister becomes an apostate to his own ordination vows. But the wisdom and power required for the church to be the church does not reside within the minister. His vision is limited. His hang-ups are real. Moreover, the minister of the local church today discovers that he is not trained sufficiently for the tasks thrust upon him through the vision that he does possess. His theological, biblical, historical training may be excellent. Yet, he discovers that this does not equip him to cope with the crunch when he seeks to put his leadership into practice.

---

[3] See John A. T. Robinson, "The Man for Others," *Honest to God* (Philadelphia: Westminster Press, 1963), pp. 64-83.

He finds large numbers in the congregation he is called to serve, who do not share his vision and hope of what the local church ought to be. When he seeks to communicate his aspirations—theologically and biblically undergirded—he seems to be talking in a foreign dialect. He is often greeted with blank faces, inertia, and then positive resistance if he insists upon pushing for the actualization of his hopes and dreams. Out of awareness of acute human need, he talks about the church reaching into the ghetto and being responsive to the human degradation that is built into the American welfare system. But talk is cheap. The word must still be made flesh. The gospel must still be incarnated. He carries his faith into the market place—protests, demonstrations and sit-ins—and all hell breaks loose within the congregation he seeks to serve and lead.

There is bewilderment and confusion on all sides. As a minister of Jesus Christ, he is simply seeking to give reality to the word he is preaching; substance to the faith he possesses. But his actions are so public and political in nature that both minister and local church immediately become the subjects of conflict and controversy. The crunch follows.

The majority of the congregation have not experienced that style of leadership; that type of challenge. The larger number, who would have been responsive, have already withdrawn, in their conviction that the local church is an archaic fossil, neither meaningful nor relevant to modern society and human needs. Those who remain have found comfort and solace in the pastoral services of their church; assurance in patterns of worship that were the same yesterday, today and hopefully forever; inspiration in preaching that stressed the personal; and fellowship in association with like-minded friends that shared their status in life, undergirded by common assumptions that were seldom if ever questioned. *Is this all wrong?* The priestly tradition of the church is long and honorable. Jesus reached out to touch men, women and children in their personal needs. His love and compassion drew all manner of people to him and he ministered to them according to their needs.

But Jesus' ministry was more than a response to individual and personal needs. It was prophetic. He was responsive to the injustices of social relationships and sharply criticized established religious practices and traditions that were insensitive to human need and perpetuated human ills rather than alleviate them. It would be difficult to find a more scathing indictment of religion than Jesus' words in Matthew 23: "Woe to you, scribes and Pharisees, hypocrites. . . ." The chapter concludes with an anguished cry of pathos:

O Jerusalem, Jerusalem, killing the prophets and stoning those who are sent to you. How often would I have gathered your children together as a hen gathers her brood under her wings, and you would not. Behold your house is forsaken and desolate.
Matthew 23:37-38

It is this same word which many feel is urgently needed in the local church . . . a word to be spoken and a word to be acted out. For some there is the dread feeling that the local church has already passed into a state of desolation.

It is this prophetic side of Christian ministry, responsive to social ills and collective human needs, that is the neglected work of the local church today. This we must do, and not leave undone the personal, pastoral services. There has been a failure to remember that Jesus was crucified, not for healing the sick, enabling the lame to walk, and pronouncing personal forgiveness to Mary Magdalene. If he had confined his ministry to such personal ministrations, all would have continued to speak well of him after the manner of the congregation of Nazareth (Luke 4:22). Jesus was crucified because he challenged the political, social, and religious structures that crushed men in body and in spirit. He was arrested and brought before Pilate for insurrection.

Jesus was well received by the congregation of Nazareth when he inspired them with his sermon of lofty hopes and aspirations:

The Spirit of the Lord is upon me,
because he has anointed me to preach good news to the poor.
He has sent me to proclaim release to the captives
and recovering of sight to the blind,
to set at liberty those who are oppressed,
to proclaim the acceptable year of the Lord.
Luke 4:18

The members of the congregation marveled and whispered with appreciation one to another. It was when he gave substance to those words that he got into trouble. He told them:

There were many widows in Israel in the days of Elijah . . . when there came a great famine over all the land; and Elijah was sent to none of them but only to Zarephath, in the land of Sidon. . . . And

> there were many lepers in Israel in the time of the prophet Elisha; and none of them was cleansed, but only Naaman the Syrian.
> Luke 4:25-27

That illustration may seem innocuous to us, but not for the congregation of Nazareth. Jesus was challenging the fundamental assertion of favoritism for the people of Israel in the sight of God. Jesus was challenging a premise upon which rested political, social and religious traditions and customs. The response of the congregation of Nazareth was swift: "They rose up and put him out of the city, and led him to the brow of the hill on which their city was built, that they might throw him down headlong (Luke 4:29)." Somehow Jesus escaped.

It is this prophetic ministry, responsive to social human needs, and a radical challenge and assault upon established customs and traditions in both church and society, that is causing such turmoil, hostility and alienation in the local church today. Neither clergy nor laity are prepared to deal adequately with the resulting pressures.

It was our mutual awareness and experience of hostility and alienation that brought us together at Laforet. Our focus was the anger, pain and fears of men and women scarred in the battles of the church. Those responsible for establishing this particular laboratory in human encounter were acutely aware that something must be done, and quickly, to enable the clergy to meet the challenge of leadership and ministry in the local church. Seminaries had not equipped their graduates for the new problems they faced. The time was already late. The flow of some of the most able and skilled leaders out of the local church was already an established pattern. Together we would seek a process and an experience that would speak to our condition as clergymen caught in the crunch. Much had been written about us, describing our dilemmas, but most of us had experienced a dearth of genuine help.

CASTING OUT DEMONS

The vehicle to express our needs was encounter groups. It is not a new method to release human potential. Educational institutions and industry have employed such techniques for two decades. Hundreds of trainees have gone through the National Training Laboratories and particular notoriety has been accorded the Esalen Institute in Big Sur, California. The press has featured T-groups and sensitivity groups—but for the most part, professional clergymen have remained untouched. During the past decade a more systematic approach has been taken by the Episcopal Church to provide opportunity for their clergymen to go through T-groups. Leadership has also been given by the Institute for Advanced Pastoral Studies in Bloomfield Hills, Michigan. Nonetheless, the implications of encounter group experiences to enable the clergyman to function more effectively have continued largely unexplored.

One continues to experience misunderstanding, apprehension, and resistance to this methodology. Leadership throughout the church is still largely premised upon authoritarian roles. Despite the rhetoric and forms of church polity, ecclesiastical roles are still primarily established through a hierarchial structure. Those who are "in" possess all the human attributes of wanting to protect their positions of power. Therefore, the act of meeting professional associates in an encounter group is a challenge to the established system of relationships. It means radical openness and radical vulnerability. It requires the willingness to be real with others, with the risks that entails. It stimulates profound anxiety. It is threatening. It means revealing your "Achilles' heel" to others, who are your professional peers and competitors, with the implication that such knowledge could be used against you. The experience of exposing one's real self runs counter to the protective instinct of masking who we are. There have been a plethora of church conferences and institutes to talk about the theological, biblical foundations of ministry with their ethical implications, but to come together to discover the deeper, personal dimensions of our identity as men and women, called to Christian ministry, represents a new experience for most. It implies a new style of leadership. It means risking the unknown. But it may also represent precisely the productive effort required to discover the kind of training needed for effective Christian ministry in the coming decades. It was this hope that brought us together. New needs bring new requirements.

The forces of resistance, however, were also in each one of us in a very personal way. Most of us shared a common conditioning, rooted in norms peculiar to the church. Rollo May provides a brilliant analysis of how the feeling side of human relationships have been atrophied in a culture that has placed such importance upon the thinking functions of man.[4] In an analytical, scientific age many of us have been conditioned to develop only one side of our personhood. Our *feeling world* has atrophied through neglect. For the clergy, this cultural conditioning, which is already very potent, is reinforced for most by a religious heritage that certain feelings are unacceptable and must be repressed. We have been brainwashed. We have been conditioned to believe that feelings of anger, pain, hostility, resentment and similar emotions are unacceptable and must not be expressed. To protect ourselves from feelings of guilt, many of us learned our lessons so well that we have been quite capable of hiding the truth from ourselves. How often I have said to myself, "I do not have such feelings." Repression blotted out reality from my own consciousness. I have no doubt that many of my peers share a similar fate.

Consciously or unconsciously, the laity reinforce this deceit by projecting upon their minister expectations of his character and behavior that frequently include a basic dishonesty in the realm of emotions and feelings. Perhaps that explains, in part, why clergymen are seen and sometimes feel like members of a third sex. The minister is expected to be nice rather than real, and it is difficult not to play "the game." That does not mean we do not experience potent feelings of anger; we simply bury them. Deep, buried emotions do not leave us unaffected. Unable to be acknowledged in a straightforward and creative way, they are spewed forth in false garb. The words of a sermon may be sweetness and light, but feeling tones of anger and hostility betray the reality of the minister's inner world. Rather than coming out direct, the potent feelings that one has been conditioned to believe were unacceptable, come out sideways. When their reality is pointed out, a prompt denial usually follows; but usually not without guilt. We cannot hide the whole truth from ourselves, and guilt and depression result. In the crunch that increasingly characterizes the life of a local church, the self-denial of his real feelings becomes increasingly difficult for any minister. How he handles these feelings becomes a critical issue for his ministry, his leadership, his integrity as a person, and his capacity for significant relationships. To continue the game of denial and repression is disastrous. I know. It is disastrous for

---

[4] Rollo May, *Love and Will* (New York: W. W. Norton & Co., 1969).

one's own personhood, and as leader of a congregation, it is equally detrimental to the health and vitality of a parish. It sanctions dishonesty and breeds guarded and false relationships at a time when openness and honesty are essential to the struggle of persons for meaning, and the quest of the church is to discover its role in a changing world.

A revealing clue came one Sunday morning when I preached a sermon on the confessions of Jeremiah. The prophet's bitter honesty stands in striking contrast to the false, sweet piety that characterizes many sermons, coating over unacknowledged and unresolved conflicts and emotions. Quoting Jeremiah's stinging accusations against God (20:7ff.), I made the following observations:

> O, how we have sentimentalized religion. We make it into something which is all sweetness and light. We use Christianity as sugar-coating over reality. In the church we give people the impression that if they really are "good Christians," they will be all smiles, all happiness, all sweetness. Nothing could be more sickening. Nothing could drive our younger generation from the church quicker than our piety which hides blood-and-guts feelings. Thank God for Jeremiah, who could call God an S.O.B.[5]

The responses of several in the congregation to this comment about Jeremiah made clear their appreciation of having their own deeper feelings legitimatized and accepted in the context of a sermon.

It was a new experience for some of us, who had come to Laforet, to be gathered about a fellow clergyman who had the honesty and courage to give expression to his deepest feelings of anger and pain. Perhaps it was not a virtue on his part; but more an experience akin to the prophet Jeremiah:

> There is in my heart as it were a burning fire
>   shut up in my bones,
> and I am weary with holding it in,
>   and I cannot.
> Jeremiah 20:9

Whatever the reason, the experience was both instructive and liberating.

It was instructive because it forced each of us to assess again our own assumptions and prejudices about our feelings. Is it

---

[5] Sermon preached in the Eliot Church, Newton, Mass., December 7, 1969.

23

true that some feelings are unacceptable and illegitimate? The answer is a clear, "no." Our feelings are our feelings. We have a right to them. By themselves they are neither good nor bad; they are simply our feelings. They are morally neutral. Angry feelings, loving feelings, sexual feelings, resentful feelings, happy feelings, jealous feelings, peaceful feelings, hurt feelings are all the same. It is what we do with them—*how we act upon them* —that makes the difference.

The disastrous, immoral thing is to deny them, however threatening they may be, for when we reject our feelings, we reject ourselves. Feelings do not evaporate; either we recognize them and deal with them openly and honestly, or we bury them, giving them the power of expression in subtle and indirect ways. Physical illnesses, psychosomatically rooted, are ways our repressed feelings get expressed. We are literally dis-eased. Through the "games people play" [6] we mask reality in our interpersonal relationships when we have not learned to handle our feelings. We become devious when we repress feelings we believe are unacceptable to others or ourselves. Sarcasm is anger expressed sideways. That is the real immorality—*not the feelings we possess*—but our inability to acknowledge them freely, and therefore, expressing them cruelly and destructively. That we are not even aware of what we are doing does not negate our sin.

The anguished cry, "I HURT," forced each of us to reflect upon the human and theological meaning of our feelings. The group leader challenged us to that reflection. The truth was transparent. In the light of the Christian gospel, that we mutually claimed to profess, there are no conditions upon our acceptability before God or man. We have a right to be loved no matter who we are or what we feel. If in the past we have experienced rejection because of our feelings—which is most apt to be grounded in self-rejection—then we have been denied our inherent, God-given right for unconditional love. We are not born into this world to meet the expectations of others. We are born to be; and that is our primary vocation before God, upon which everything else depends. That truth finds particular expression in the prayer of Gestalt Therapy:

I do my thing, and you do your thing.
I am not in this world to live up to your expectations

---

[6] Eric Berne, *The Games People Play* (New York: Grove Press, 1964).

And you are not in this world to live up to mine.
You are you and I am I,
And if by chance we find each other, it's beautiful.
If not, it can't be helped.[7]

This confrontation with an expression of gut feelings was indeed instructive, but also liberating. It gave others of us the courage to take a more honest look at ourselves—to risk lifting the lid on our inner world. What spewed forth in the 24-hour marathon that initiated our ten days together was a clear documentation of the pain, hurt, anger and deeply repressed feelings being carried by clergymen today. Surely we were no exception. As ministers of Christ, we needed liberation from our own bondage, that we might be free to minister to others.

MINISTER IN NEED

The learning experience—the uninhibited sharing of our whole selves with one another—was unquestionably a new, isolated experience for most of us. What it could mean "back home" with the congregations we served, the people with whom we shared our daily lives, was still a question to be answered. Could we risk being our real selves with those who looked to us as their ministers? Would members of our congregations accept us as ordinary human beings, seeking to serve Christ, with our protective role images stripped away? Could the conditioning process that has defined the minister's role give way to a more honest relationship?

It was some months before these questions would be put to the test in my personal ministry. The occasion was the decision of the United States government to invade Cambodia in the spring of 1970.

For several years I had identified myself with various anti-war activities. The war in Vietnam was a fundamental moral issue for me, requiring concrete expression, if I was to maintain integrity in my Christian life-style. I was a veteran of the European theater of operations during World War II, and never classified myself a pacifist, but I found myself totally opposed to American involvement in Vietnam. If, indeed there were high ideals and motives for the United States to go to war in Indochina at

---

[7] Frederick S. Perls, *Gestalt Therapy Verbatim* (Lafayette, Calif.: Real People Press, 1969), p. 4.

the outset; the nature of my country's military action had obliterated all altruistic intentions. Historians may well point to My Lai as the symbol of the American presence in Vietnam or quote the American officer, who, viewing the rubble of a Vietnamese village, said, "We had to destroy it in order to save it."

For me, Christian morality required a personal response. I accepted responsibility as chairman of the Boston chapter of Clergy and Laymen Concerned About Vietnam. I participated in many public demonstrations against the war both locally and in Washington, D.C. I took a stand with those who destroyed their draft cards as an act of personal conscience. I had preached from the pulpit of the Eliot Church against the war with as much moral persuasion as possible. I had sought to bring the biblical, theological insights of the Christian faith to bear upon this particular world event, in the conviction that if God so loved the world that he was willing to act through Christ; then the church had best take world events seriously.

Then on April 30, 1970, President Nixon announced that the war in southeast Asia had been expanded and American military forces had invaded Cambodia. What more could I say? What else could I do? *The force of the President's announcement disabled me physically, emotionally and spiritually.* Three days later I would be expected to lead another service of worship for the congregation I served.

On Saturday I told my wife that I could not go through with it on Sunday morning. Over many months I had piled words upon words seeking to relate in a meaningful way the Christian faith to personal and public issues. The event of Cambodia left me exhausted. I had nothing left to say. I informed two deacons of the church of my condition.

I came to the hour of worship on Sunday morning not knowing what I would say or do. The order of service was printed in the usual format. It had been prepared and printed before the President's announcement. The service of worship began in the customary manner. When it came time for the sermon I went to the pulpit, and in a few halting words tried to tell those present that I could not speak. World events had choked off my words. I concluded with Jesus' words, "Blessed are the peacemakers, for they shall be called sons of God (Matt. 5:9)," and added that if there was an equivalent in our culture of the biblical sack cloth and ashes, that would be my chosen attire in the face of this na-

26

tional disaster. I invited anyone who had anything to say to me or to other members of the congregation to do so. I took off my black robe, draped it across the pulpit, and seated myself on the chancel steps.

In the moments that followed I remember one or two voices speaking from the congregation, but almost immediately their words were lost in the torrent of emotions that welled up from within myself and overwhelmed me. When I became aware again, I realized that many members of the congregation were seated around me in the chancel. I heard their words. I felt their touch. Their love and concern encapsulated me.

After some minutes I said, "Thank you. I think I can function again." One woman responded, "I thought when you laid your robe on the pulpit, you were renouncing your ministry." I assured her that my Christian faith was still real, but that I had become disfunctional, momentarily, by the overpowering trauma of the Cambodian invasion. Their presence in the chancel with me, their love and concern for me, were calling me back to life and to my ministry again.

The suggestion to close the service with a simple hymn was rejected. One person stated that what had happened was in the context of our experience of worship and that the service should be completed as planned. Prayers were spoken, the offering was taken with people making their contributions from their places on the steps of the chancel and the floor of the sanctuary. Never did Haydn's anthem, "Great and Glorious," as sung by the choir, sound more uplifting. Prior to the benediction, one family announced they would like to go home, gather the food they had planned for dinner, and return to the church. Would others like to join them?

At 2:00 p.m., more than 50 members had gathered in the fellowship hall of the church. The food was placed on the table and we broke bread together. It was an *agape feast* that fed body and soul. From the tables we moved into a circle, and after singing together and offering prayers, a loaf was passed and a common chalice.

It was 5:30 p.m. before the conversation ceased, but, then, only momentarily. Much attention had centered on the question, "What can we do?" Were we simply to share in a cathartic experience, a fellowship of concern, and go our separate ways? A smaller group decided they would come together that evening and hammer out specific proposals to set before the whole group. Seventeen gathered at 8:30 P.M., broke into task forces, and worked out three specific courses of action. The first would be to center the service of worship on May 31 around the concept of the "Global Village" and the urgent need for world development. The second group worked on legislative issues and the need to redouble one's efforts to express moral concerns and outrage through the political process. The third group planned a protest against the expansion of the war in Indochina that would take place on the lawn of the church. The latter was the most radical proposal of all.

In conservative, affluent Newton, such public action by a church would be unprecedented. But the Spirit moves in wondrous ways, and it is in "the moments of darkness" that new opportunities for life present themselves. The church today knows pain and death, but it can also experience life and joy. Following the crucifixion, there is resurrection—but one can never be sure. It only comes through an act of faith—to those who say, "Father, into thy hands I commit my spirit (Luke 23:46)."

The executive committee of the church, charged with the responsibility for the use of church property, was scheduled to hold its monthly meeting the following night. Monday evening, 30 members of the church, who had convened in the fellowship hall the prior afternoon, waited upon the executive committee to make their request. Would they be allowed, as church members, to make their Christian witness in a public way on the lawn of the church? Many members of the church would not agree with such a demonstration. Was the breadth of fellowship wide enough to tolerate such diversity? Lively discussion followed the request. Loss of members, cutting off of funds, and potential damage to the property all had their airing, and then the vote was taken. The answer was, yes, with two dissenting votes. The decision was made to allow a group of church members the privilege of bearing public witness to their faith, and to give expression on church property to their moral outrage over a particular national event, *despite the possible institutional consequences to the church.* How ironical that Christians must struggle for the privilege of being Christian within the church today. How illuminating of the value system that preoccupies the church. The albatross that hangs around the neck of the Christian church is its property. It may yet prove to be the millstone that drowns it.

To test the preoccupation of a local church with its property, compare the response of church members to meetings called for the purposes of education or service, and those called to make decisions regarding finances and property. Secular man knows where the action is. And woe to the minister who is taken in by the assurances of a board of trustees, or similar body, that they will take responsibility for all financial matters, thereby freeing him to attend to religious and spiritual matters. Power is with the purse string in or out of the church. Budget and building use are the channels through which the religious, spiritual convictions of the church are made real. When a church excludes from membership persons of a minority race; when it prohibits its own members or community groups from using portions of its facilities for fear of dirtying the rug or marring the furniture; when it spends lavishly on its own ecclesiastical appointments— all to the glory of God—and gives a pittance, by comparison, to the mission, outreach work of the church; *then it tells it like it is, a message that no one can miss.* The uses of money and property by the church is a theme that will weave itself throughout the chapters of this book, for decisions in these two areas reveal priorities and commitments.

Tuesday, following the affirmative decision of the night before, was a day of spontaneous and feverish activity, and at 7:00 A.M., Wednesday, May 6, 1970, 35 members of the congregation gathered on the front steps of the Eliot Church for a service of worship to initiate a daily vigil that would last for eight weeks. A casket draped with an American flag—the tragic symbol of America in the eyes of the world—was carried from the sanctuary and placed on a table on the lawn to be surrounded by men, women and children from the church, who were bearing witness to their faith and convictions that this madness in Southeast Asia must cease.

This action by church members tells its own story, but behind it is revealed a profound lesson for me as a minister of a local church. I began with the question, can a minister risk being real with church members who look up to him, who expect certain things of him? This is compounded by the expectations we have learned to lay upon ourselves as ministers of the gospel of Christ. There is the anticipation that we will always be strong, adequate and giving. That illusion was publically shattered before the congregation of the Eliot Church on a particular May morning in 1970. But what has taken its place is a reality far more meaningful than the phantasy of perfection which is debilitating many ministers and assuring a dishonesty of relationships with their parishioners.

Ordination to the Christian ministry does not transport any person into another category of human experience. Needs, emotions, feelings remain the same. The basic dishonesty of Christian ministry today is that many of us have been programmed into pretending that we are different than ordinary mortals, and many members of our congregations play that game, so that they can live vicariously through us. But, thank God, for me the truth is out. I stand before the congregation I serve as a man in need, like everyone else. In responding to my needs, both on a particular Sunday morning described above, and since, I have learned a good deal more what the Christian gospel is all about, and am better equipped to be a minister of Jesus Christ.

Chapter 2
CHURCH IN THE CRUNCH

Everywhere we look in the church the threshold of pain is very high. No one escapes, for at all levels of the church's life, we are no longer in the midst of orderly transition; we are being catapulted into revolutionary changes. In the institutional church everything that is not nailed down is in motion, and in the particular church I serve, even the pews of the sanctuary are being unscrewed to make way for new forms of contemporary worship. Viewing the front pews of the sanctuary now placed sideways, one long-time member of the church muttered contemptuously, "Sacrilegious!"

Are the fixed, ecclesiastical forms the unshakable foundations upon which the church rests, and against which the gates of hell shall not prevail? Or are the church's immovable foundations resting upon other pillars? Changes are necessary, indeed, inevitable. But what changes? To what drumbeat shall we march? What piper shall we follow? Colin W. Williams, Dean of the Yale Divinity School, reminds us that when Luther celebrated his first mass, his father, who had objected to his becoming a monk, came to him and said:

> Martin, you should not have been here. Don't you know that God said that you have to obey your father?

Luther responded:

> But I heard a word from God—a higher word—and he told me that I must enter the monastery.

To which the father replied:

> How do you know it wasn't the devil? [1]

---

[1] "The Church Responds." An address by Colin W. Williams to the Pre-Assembly Conference on Evangelism, The United Presbyterian Church, U.S.A., May 1966, Boston, Mass., p. 9.

That is the question that plagues many of us in the church. We push for change in the name of serving the Lord, and in order to make the church more relevant to human needs. But what changes are in keeping with the will of God? Are we open to the leading of the Spirit, or are we driven by ego needs? There is no certain answer. Time alone will test our work, sifting out what is of man and transient, and what is of God and enduring. My effort will be simply to chronicle some of the experiences that reveal the pain and joy of ministry and in later chapters to draw out their implications for new forms of ministry, leadership development and organizational changes within the church.

THE LOCAL CHURCH

The action by approximately 50 members of the Eliot Church to hold a public demonstration on the front lawn of the church created a crisis both within the church and community. Polarization, for and against, took place immediately. It reflected the mood of the nation as colleges and high schools closed down through student strikes, while other voices called for "patriotic support" of the President's decision to invade Cambodia.

During the initial days, the protest action and Christian witness was held 12 hours each day. Members of the church were joined by scores of others in the community who welcomed an opportunity to give witness to their outrage and indignation. This channel of action became even more significant following the death of students at Kent State and Jackson State Universities. Facilities were provided for citizens to send telegrams to the President and other public officials. As an additional educational vehicle, the film, "Hiroshima-Nagasaki," was shown every hour in the narthex of the church. A local junior high school availed themselves of this opportunity by sending classes to the church to view the film.

Needless to say, the demonstration precipitated other kinds of responses. A church member, whose son was in Vietnam, immediately withdrew his membership and another member expressed her anguish by writing that henceforth her pew in the church would be vacant. The first Sunday morning following the beginning of the demonstration, the casket, draped with the American flag, was on the lawn of the church, flanked by the senior deacon and senior deaconess. Some members of the church drove up to the curb, looked, and drove away. In subsequent conversations they revealed that they simply could not associate such action with the worship of God. Here is the matrix of the tension that exists within the Christian community. It is centered upon our understanding of the role of the church.

Again I turn to Colin Williams to illuminate the issue:

> The story that Matthew has is of people from the Church coming up to heaven on the last day and knocking on the door, and Christ opens it up and says to them, "Yes, Who are you?" And they say, "Oh, we're all Presbyterians. We've just been to our General Assembly and you blew the trumpet and we've come, ready to enter." And the story says, Christ will look you in the eye and say, "Oh, sorry, I didn't recognize you." And the Presbyterians will say, "This is no time for joking, Lord—you know that we have done many wonderful works in your name. We've kept churches going all over the country—we've had big Sunday Schools—we've run stewardship campaigns—we've done wonderful things in your name." And he'll say to you, "I'm sorry—I've never seen you before. For I was in prison, but you were so busy running the Church you never got there. I was naked—you were so occupied in your internal church life that you never saw the needs of the world. I was thirsty, and you were so busy about letting the church be spiritual and telling the Church to keep out of secular affairs that you missed me altogether."
>
> Here then, is a simple statement to the Church: *That if the Church concentrates on its inner life it is no longer the Church of Jesus Christ* [italics added]. Unless the Church is free to respond to Christ's presence in the world, continuing what he was doing when he was on earth, and calling us to be with him at the places where he is meeting the world's needs; unless the Church is free for the work of Christ in the world, free to listen to the world in such a way that it hears what Christ is saying from the world, unless the Church is free for that it's not an evangelical Church at all.[2]

The most immediate and serious negative response, however, came the first day in a confrontation with members of a local post of the American Legion. There was momentary violence, but no serious injury. Four men snatched the American flag from the coffin and in the scuffle that ensued, a seven-year-old girl was knocked to the ground, and the senior deacon of the church was dragged into the street and suffered minor facial lacerations. All this took place while a police officer in a traffic control cruiser watched, and did nothing. After a vigorous protest to local police officials, as well as political leaders of the com-

---

[2] Ibid., pp. 8-9.

munity, the church flag "mysteriously" appeared behind a store across the street from the church and was returned by the police. No formal complaint was filed regarding the theft and the chief of police of the city of Newton promised any protection that was requested by the church. No request was made and no further violence occurred during the eight weeks of the demonstration. A counter demonstration was held, however, by members of the Legion post. The Legionnaire, who led that action, is also a member of the Eliot Church, and remains so to the present time.

Because of widespread publicity given by both newspapers and television to this particular visible and public religious witness, and the participation of many citizens in the community, the following Statement of Purpose was drafted by those who originated the protest demonstration:

> We protest the invasion of Cambodia by the United States and the enlargement of the war in Southeast Asia.
>
> We mourn the dead—more than 800,000—from Vietnam to the campus of Kent State University [this Statement was issued before the student deaths at Jackson State] and have placed an American flag on a symbolic coffin to express our deep anguish.
>
> We are ashamed that for many the Stars and Stripes have now become a symbol around the world of repression, death, and destruction. We believe the flag of our nation has been desecrated by our government's policies and actions.
>
> At the same time, we proudly carry the flag of our country as a sign of our hope that our great nation can once again become a symbol to all of honor, freedom, justice, and peace.
>
> We have gathered from many churches and synagogues in the community, but do not speak for any religious institution. We simply witness to the personal convictions and moral values of our religious faith.
>
> *We invite you to stand with us.*

The Statement was released to the news media and given as handouts to the hundreds of commuters who passed the church each day. After the first two weeks, it was determined to continue the vigil only during the heavy hours of commuter traffic in the morning and late afternoon.

How does one assess the impact of such an event upon the life of a local congregation? What criteria determine decisions within the Christian community? Responses to the demonstration upon the church lawn were immediate, intense, and reflected very diverse judgments. On May 27, 1970—in the midst of the witness by church members against American military ac-

tion in Cambodia—the membership of Eliot Church convened
for the annual spring congregational meeting. It was impossible
to conduct business as usual. As minister of Eliot Church, I requested the opportunity to make the following observations:

I have asked for a few moments this evening to set an issue before
you which is of great personal concern to me and has direct bearing upon the considerations of many for the future of this church.

Since May 6, 1970, the vigil and protest being held daily on the
front lawn of the Eliot Church have prompted much comment—
both supportive and critical. That comes as no surprise. Our church
and the city of Newton are as divided as the nation on the issue
of the Indo-China War.

What does concern me, however, are the foundations upon which
many of the comments have been made. Let me state the obvious.
We are a Christian Church. Therefore, the criteria by which our
decisions are made, as a Christian fellowship, must have their roots
in our Biblical/theological heritage. I did not say our decisions
ought to be so grounded; I did not say it would be nice to employ
such criteria if the world were only more amenable to Christian
ideals; I repeat, our basic, fundamental decisions must be grounded
in the heritage of our faith, if we are to be a Christian church.

Christians, who make their Biblical/theological heritage the foundation for determining their actions, can honestly differ. We see
this in the book of Acts in the controversy between Peter and
Paul. But the yardstick of measurement is unalterable. It is not
prudential considerations; it is not personal opinions; it is not offensiveness to others; it is not institutional survival that determine
what Christians do or do not do—it is a matter of being faithful
to our Biblical/theological faith, as best we understand it. Christians
are called to be obedient to the teachings of Jesus Christ, and let
the chips fall where they may.

During the past month, the action taken by members of this
church to hold a demonstration on the church lawn against the
Cambodian War has been criticized because it allegedly gives aid
and comfort to the enemy, or because it is offensive to the sensibilities of some members of the church or citizens of the community, or because it will undercut the financial support of this church.
Not one of these arguments carries substantial weight or has ultimate
validity within a Christian church. The roots of decision-making are
much deeper.

If Eliot Church is a Church of Jesus Christ, then this church does
not belong to us—no matter how much money we have spent supporting it or how much time we have invested in its work. This
church belongs to Christ and no one else. Its future is in his hands
and not ours. We are called to carry on his ministry and make our
decisions for action, based upon our understanding of his will and
purpose. Anything less is unfaithfulness.

Any action taken by a group of church members is open to criti-
cism, and we will all be more faithful to our Christian vocation
when we are in continual, and sometimes tense, interaction with
one another. I simply remind you tonight that the foundations of
our actions and our criticisms must be our Biblical/theological heri-

tage. Other arguments are null and void in the Christian Church however valid they may be in the secular world.

In 1916, Woodrow Wilson wrote, "A point in national affairs never lies along the lines of expediency. It always rests in the field of principle." These are the ground rules within the Christian Church: when the moment of critical decision comes, neither expediency, nor offensiveness, nor institutional considerations have merit. It is our Biblical/theological foundations that provide the plumb line.

The shock and anger this particular action brought to some members of the church were revealed more fully in the fall of 1970—and were combined with a response to another event. Newton is located within the Third Congressional District of Massachusetts, which was the center of a political primary that drew national attention. The Democratic incumbent, Congressman Philip J. Philbin, the second-ranking member of the House Armed Services Committee, was being opposed by Father Robert Drinan, Dean of the Boston College Law School. Father Drinan was an outspoken critic of the Vietnam War.

During the past years community groups have used the facilities of the Eliot Church for many purposes. Therefore, when a request was received for the use of the church building for a political rally in support of the candidacy of Father Drinan, permission was granted. One could find many precedents in the long history of New England Congregationalism in having a local church used as a community center for political purposes. *No endorsement was sought or given by the church to the candidate.* The request was treated as one more desire of a community organization to use the church facilities. *However, it was not so interpreted by some church members,* and in hindsight, one might say that the reactions that ensued might have been anticipated, and possibly would have changed the decision in the use of the church building by a political candidate.

The reaction to the demonstration the preceding May and the permission given to Father Drinan to use the church building provoked the following protest petition, with a hundred signatures, which was formally presented to the executive committee at their meeting in September 1970.[3]

As members of Eliot Church of Newton, we wish to register our disapproval of the use of the church premises for partisan political

---

[3] Nineteen signers of the petition were either not members of the church or had not participated in the life of the church for at least 10 years.

purposes. Currently a rally for a candidate in the Third Massachusetts District for Congress, Father Drinan, is being advertised.

Our reaction is not based on the party affiliation of Mr. Drinan. We would consider it equally inappropriate to use the church grounds to promote a candidate of the opposing party.

All of us contributed our efforts and substance to the rebuilding of a graceful edifice, dedicated first and foremost to the worship of God, and set apart for that purpose. There was also provision for religious education and a place for gatherings designed for the traditional role of the Congregational Church to reconcile the conflicts and friction within our community by consideration of our common problems in an atmosphere of good will and neighborliness, as children of one God, where a true consensus could be sought under the guidance of the Holy Spirit. These never included partisan politics.[*1]

Unhappily we have found that, rather than seeking to learn the views of the rank and file, a militant group has made use of the premises for demonstrations calculated to offend the sensibilities of a large segment of the membership and of the community—as in the display of casket and flag—used in opposition to the Government's sweep against Viet Cong bases in the Cambodian jungle last May.

We regret that the aggressive managers of these partisan acts fail to realize that they are counter-productive, in that the shy person who needs time for reflection, who wishes to consider all sides, is repelled by these strident demands. These persons are often the people who need the church most, but are now alienated.

Despite the perfunctory denials, we cannot escape the feeling that the church grounds have been chosen for these demonstrations partly to give the impression that they represent the considered views of the membership as a whole. This is not the fact. As long time members and supporters of Eliot Church we wish to emphasize that the rank and file were not consulted about this radical change in policy and we wish to disassociate ourselves from it. We also note that this jeopardizes the tax exemption of all contributions to the church.[**2]

NOTE[*1] Several members of Eliot have held political office in recent years. Edwin O. Childs, Theodore Lockwood and Donald Gibbs were Mayors of Newton. Richard Lee and Donald Gibbs were Senators, George Rawson was State Representative. None of these ever used the facilities of the church in their campaigns.

NOTE[**2] The U.S. Internal Revenue Code gives tax exemption for contributions to institutions "operated exclusively for religious, charitable . . . or educational purposes" . . . "No substantial part of the activities of which is carrying on propaganda or otherwise attempting to influence legislation and which does not participate in . . . any political campaign on behalf of any candidate for public office."

The Hatfield-McGovern resolution on Vietnam was pending in Congress at the time of the casket demonstration at Eliot Church.

Father Drinan's candidacy was approaching the primary election when his rally was held.

A brief, formal response was sent by the executive committee to all signers of the petition, but in no way was it adequate
to deal with the substantive issues raised. One must also remember that events at the Eliot Church in 1970 followed upon many
other efforts of the church to respond to human needs and
worldly events. These are recorded in *Conflict and Change in
the Church*.[4] Subsequently, a letter of invitation was extended to
all those who signed the petition to meet with the executive
committee at their December meeting. Only six signatories appeared. Many words were spoken, but one was not left with the
impression that communication took place. The premises of the
arguments on both sides were so fundamentally different that a
common meeting ground appeared impossible—at least for the
moment. The differences were sharply illuminated in the following letter sent to the clerk of the church's executive committee
by a signer of the protest petition:

December 1, 1970

Mrs. Elizabeth B. Merrill, Clerk
The Eliot Church of Newton
474 Centre Street, Newton, Massachusetts 02158

Dear Betty:

Let me acknowledge your letter of November 9th sent to me and
the other ninety-nine signers of the petition of last September, inviting us to attend the December 7th meeting of the Executive
Committee. I doubt the value of such a meeting at this time.

I think that the text of the petition speaks for itself, but I might
add an individual comment in the light of your letter. The issues of
the petition go deeper than a mere diversity of interests often referred
to as pluralism. If it were just a question as to the type of worship
service, guitar music vs. pipe organ, or contemporary vs. conventional
liturgy, the problem could be solved by alternating or having both in
separate places. If it were a matter of assisting the Fernald School or
an Indian Reservation, we could establish priorities. Those are problems of pluralism.

The actions protested in the September petition were partisan
political activities of a type never before indulged in, in the one
hundred twenty-five year existence of Eliot Church, nor by any other
churches in the neighborhood. They divide the community on partisan
lines, in a manner which brings out the worst in people on both sides.

The American public believes deeply that our way of life is wor-
thy of great sacrifice and gives unstinting honor to those who fall in
its service, whether it be patrolman Schroeder in Brighton, or John
Doe in Vietnam. Generations of Americans have been stirred by
Lincoln's words—"that from these honored dead, we take increased
devotion" . . . "It is for us the living . . . to be dedicated to the

---

[4] Harold R. Fray, Jr., *Conflict and Change in the Church* (Philadelphia: Pilgrim Press, 1969).

unfinished work" . . . "which they have thus far so nobly advanced."
The flag and coffin display on Eliot's lawn appeared to be an attempt
to dishonor the dead and to shame their sacrifice.

Reasonable men can well debate whether the policies of the present administration are the best ways to achieve world peace, and
self determination for our allies. That is open to argument. But a
mock funeral casts aspersions on the symbol of our national ideals,
and impugns the motives of those who died in its service. It offends
without persuading.

Using the church grounds for a rally for a candidate for congress,
when there are other suitable sites, indicates greater interest in our
father who art in congress than in the Father in Heaven to whom
the edifice was dedicated.

The other point raised by the petition was the disregard of the
democratic principles of our denomination in expropriating the church
premises for these purposes. So far as I can learn, no vote was ever
taken by the church as a whole authorizing either of these political
acts. An article in the Boston Herald Traveler reports that a sort of
ad hoc decision was made by members who attended a Sunday
service in May—before the flag and coffin display. As for the September rally, there was not even a discussion or vote in the Executive
Committee authorizing it. Elaborate study, discussion and notice to
all members was the procedure before Eliot Church voted to join the
United Church—and later the United Parish in Newton, but the
political commitments which we protested were arranged by a few
insiders without consulting the membership. Such manipulation
weakens the voice of the church for the future. It is, however, a fait
accompli, and there seems no point in a meeting to review the past.

I regret the need for spelling out what I had thought was obvious.
I assume that the persons who took the protested action did not
realize that so many of their fellow members would be so deeply
offended, but I can but wonder why they did not inquire before
acting.

Before I close this long letter, let me make one other point. It is
not the people who circulated the September petition, nor those who
signed it, who have divided the church. The exodus had begun
before then, and many persons who were like-minded had either
severed their connections, or did not choose to sign. The petition did
call attention to the deep division.

It is ironic that the proposal for a meeting should issue at the
same time as the appeal for financial contributions. To paraphrase
an old song—

"Did you love me in May
    As you seem to do in December?"

I hope that some reconciling and constructive result can come
from this airing of views that you have invited, and that in the
future the church can avoid ill will and be sensitive to the feelings
and hopes of all its members and neighbors.

Sincerely,

Dick Lee [5]

---

[5] Richard H. Lee, a long-time member of Eliot Church, has served
as moderator of the church and member of the board of trustees in
recent years. At one time he was a State Senator from Newton.

At this crossroad of wide differences, suspicion and mistrust lies the pain of a Christian community seeking to respond to the moral dilemmas of our time, and discovering an internal brokenness and alienation that seem insurmountable at the moment. Understandably one could ask: is it worth it? To what does Christ call us today?

One additional fact should be cited for its possible bearing upon the hurt being experienced by many older members of Eliot Church. The church edifice was destroyed by fire in February 1956, and a new building was erected and dedicated in December 1957—at a cost of $800,000. Of that amount $240,000 was realized from the insurance on the former building, while citizens and organizations within the Newton community contributed another $60,000. That still required members of the church to pay $500,000 for the new edifice, in addition to financing the annual budgets of the church. The indebtedness for the new building was amortized in 5 years, and the last note was formally burned in December 1962—which was the occasion for my reception as the new minister of the Eliot Church of Newton.

The changes that have occurred within the church during the past decade, the ascendancy of new leadership to boards and committees, the influx of new members—many of whom joined for the expressed purpose of identifying with the particular ministries of the Eliot Church—have left many older members with the conviction that their church, which they paid for, has been taken from them. On numerous occasions this feeling has been verbalized. It is expressed through the protest petition:

> All of us contributed our efforts and substance to the rebuilding of a graceful edifice, dedicated first and foremost to the worship of God, and set apart for that purpose.

Many cannot, and perhaps will never understand that it is precisely the worship of God that prompts the actions that have been characteristic of the Eliot Church during the decade of the 60's. One former member expressed his anger and frustration by requesting that memorial gifts which he had given to the church at the time it was rebuilt, be returned to him. His request was honored.

Now let us examine how these same events refract a different light for other members and people within the community. The events are the same, but the responses emerge out of another center.

Perhaps the most significant, visible reward for those church members who actively engaged in the Cambodian demonstration was the new sense of community and support. Those most actively involved met daily at the supper hour for the first two weeks to assess the day's events and plan for the morrow. There was created a sense of community and identity that had never been experienced by many through years of personal involvement in the church. One member said, "After sixty years I no longer feel alone in my concerns." Furthermore, it provided a channel of action. Another man said, "I think that if I did not have some vehicle through which to express my anger and frustration, I would have exploded." One can surely argue the merits of such a demonstration in affecting public policy, but the personal benefits to many participants were a demonstrated fact.

How clearly this was revealed at the Sunday morning service of worship that followed the initiation of the demonstration. The time normally devoted to the sermon became the occasion for those who were participants in the demonstration to share with others the meaning of the week's events. A moving witness was made by a mother who had grown up in the Eliot Church and was the wife of a career Navy officer. When she spoke, those in the congregation strained to catch every word:

> My purpose here this morning is not to hold forth on why the war is offensive to the world as well as ourselves and a dishonor to us. Those subjects have been publically and extensively before us in Eliot Church for some time and handled so well.
>
> Instead I present myself to you as a dissenter who cannot be dismissed on the usual grounds, for I am not one of the "Young," I am not a student or a part of adult academia. I am not a bum nor an effete intellectual snob, nor a violence-espousing revolutionary, or angry or whatever term is being used currently to render dissenters rejectionable, to castrate their effect.
>
> I am 33 years old (just); the wife of a 20-year career Navy officer and make my dissent with a heavy heart because, in addition to mourning with all of you the loss of human lives and the spoilage of land, to suffering from the divisiveness over the war throughout America,—in addition to this, my own family is being and has been divided over the war in a painful way. I have passed from frustration, to anger, and since the Cambodian decision, to intensified sorrow and foreboding, but not fortunately, a sense of futility and complete helplessness.
>
> I am speaking out because I feel that in my position as a semimilitary wife, I have an even greater responsibility than the aver-

REGIS
BIBL. MAJ.
COLLEGE

age civilian to evaluate our military behavior and act on my convictions as to our moral duty. Even though my husband is only semi-military in that he is not a line officer but rather on Engineering Duty Only, I am still technically part of the military.

Right or wrong, I feel my time has come to stand up for the count in every peaceful way I can. Aware as I am that there is no complete moral rectitude for any of us, my mind and heart are strongly against this war and this is where I want to stand. This standing up so publically for the count is long overdue for me. I feel like the hypothetical woman who is 12 months pregnant and her time has finally come. For me, the time for sporadic and mostly private clucking and handwringing is over and I feel impelled by conscience and heart to protest this war in whatever peaceful means available to me.

Let me say clearly—I am not speaking for any other military wife except myself. I just don't know their feelings conclusively—there is too much silence.

There are more and more of us non-stereotyped dissenters emerging actively, our hour comes at last. I hope the hour comes very soon for the rest of us—inside these walls and without. I hope it is not already too late to prevent greatly increased war tragedy.[6]

An additional rare moment came the following Sunday morning when again members of the church were gathered on the lawn prior to the worship service. As they clustered around the casket draped with the flag, with a 10-foot wooden cross a few feet behind them, a car drove up to the curb and a man beckoned one of the church members to come over to him. When he did so, the man thrust a box at him through the open window of the car and immediately drove off. Upon opening it, the box was found to contain a Bronze Star and a Military Merit medal. An attached note read:

Please accept these. I earned them in Vietnam but cannot, in good conscience, keep them.

The box containing the medals were brought to the altar of the church at the time the offerings of the congregation were received.

An equally dramatic event occurred some days later. I received a telephone call from a man with whom I had shared in various peace activities. He is a Roman Catholic layman from a neighboring community. He asked if we could have lunch together. I agreed, and during our luncheon, he spoke of the great appreciation shared by his wife and him for the peace actions of the Eliot Church. He said that they were particularly moved by

---

[6] Statement by Mrs. Barbara Riddell at the service of worship of the Eliot Church of Newton, May 10, 1970.

those members of the church who were engaged in the demonstration protesting U.S. expansion of the war in Indochina. Then he asked, "Would it be possible for them to make a contribution of $1,000 to the peace work of Eliot Church?" I assured him, it could be handled. Understandably the impact upon those engaged in the demonstration was electric when I reported my conversation and this man's generous offer. I remembered the words of the hymn, which we had sung in the church many times, "God moves in a mysterious way, his wonders to perform." And I recalled the conversation of the church executive committee when we debated the propriety of using the church lawn for this particular form of Christian witness. Questions had been raised, with fear and trembling, regarding loss of members, the cutting off of financial support, and potential damage to the church property.

True, there has been a loss of financial contributions from some members, and though very few have actually withdrawn their membership, some are conspicuous by their absence from all church functions. At the same time new members have joined the church in a deliberate response to the church's action. A couple, who planned to move to Newton from a community on the north shore of Massachusetts, drove by Eliot Church, and seeing the demonstration, said to themselves without any personal acquaintance with the church, "When we move to Newton, that is the church we are going to join." And they have.

Finally, I would cite a less dramatic, but no less moving experience that deeply touched many of us. Adjacent to the church is an apartment house, where several members of Eliot Church reside. One of them is a widow, 87 years old at the time, a member of the church for many, many years. Understandably she was troubled and uncertain by all that was happening at her church. She felt deep pain over the harsh remarks of her contemporaries regarding the church and the peace action on the lawn. She brooded about it, and after two weeks had passed, she appeared one afternoon and said she would like to join the demonstration. A chair was brought from the church for her to sit in, and then she pressed into my hand a poem she had written—in the style of a Japanese Haiku:

> Just eighteen—too young
> To vote. Can it be God's will
> Old enough to kill? [7]

---

[7] Written by Viola Bosdan.

After that, she was seated among the demonstrators many after-noons.

There is no answer to the dilemmas facing the institutional church squeezed in the crunch. Within the church, "One man's meat, is another man's poison." We can only humbly acknowledge that the church belongs to Christ, and we leave the ultimate outcome in his hands as we seek to be faithful through this difficult period that is given to us. The same problems reverberate through all areas of the church's life. I now turn the spotlight on other arenas of action. Again we will discover that the pain is massive, but the joy is also very real. The cycle of death and resurrection within the church continue to manifest themselves as the central symbols of faith. What is happening at the state and national levels of the church's life also has fundamental implications for organizational changes and leadership development—topics which shall occupy our attention in later chapters.

THE MASSACHUSETTS STORY

It began in the summer of 1969—at least in its visible manifestation. One can never trace the roots of a leap of faith—a bold, dramatic decision—that catapults the church, in this instance the Massachusetts Conference of the United Church of Christ, into an arena of action destined to change its very life style and to confront the 531 conference churches with opportunities and controversies unprecedented in recent years. The seeds of faith that blossom into hard, bold decisions are known only to God. But it can be said that for some members of the board of directors of the conference it was related to convictions, conscience, and the painful awareness of white racism, as documented by the President's Commission on Civil Disorders (known as the Kerner Report).[8]

On August 7, 1969, the Directors of the Massachusetts Council of Churches took action to fund—at an annual rate of $35,000 for five years—a Black Ecumenical Commission. This action dissolved the Council's three-year-old race commission, in recognition of the new commission being formed under the leadership of the Metropolitan Boston Committee of Black Churchmen, for

---

[8] *Report of the National Advisory Commission on Civil Disorders* (New York: E. P. Dutton & Co., 1968).

the purpose of "empowerment, unity and self-determination of the black people" in the Commonwealth of Massachusetts.

During this same period those in positions of leadership within the Massachusetts Conference of the United Church of Christ pondered what action would be appropriate to meet these same critical needs of black empowerment and self-determination. For years the conference had proclaimed the appropriate words of brotherhood and justice through annual resolutions, but what action would give substance to the rhetoric? The answer was forthcoming, not many weeks after the August 1969 decision of the Directors of the State Council. On October 8, 1969, the conference directors voted to give one million dollars of conference assets to the Black Ecumenical Commission that was in the process of formation. That represented one fourth of the conference's endowment funds, and the total resources of the conference not restricted by terms of the trusts. On October 9, a letter was sent to all conference churches informing them of this decision. That was just 10 days prior to a scheduled recessed annual meeting of the conference at which a vote would be taken to elect a new conference minister and president, the Rev. Avery D. Post.

The news of the board's action penetrated the conference churches like shock waves, and precipitated the whole range of predictable reactions—amazement, shock, anger, elation, joy, celebration. Overnight members of the United Church of Christ within the state, who hardly knew that a State Conference existed, let alone what it did, suddenly discovered a new ecclesiastical entity, that had been around for 170 years. By Saturday, October 18, when the conference convened its recessed annual meeting in Worcester, Massachusetts, sides were already being drawn. It was the first exposure of the candidate for president to the business affairs of the conference, and he summarized the day's events as "an ecclesiastical shoot-out."

As the gavel came down to open the meeting, a motion was made to change the printed agenda in order that delegates might consider action that would have instructed the conference directors "to defer the implementation of their October 8 commitment." This proposal already had the support of 180 ministers who had signed a statement prior to the meeting, which questioned whether the directors' action had impaired "the integrity of Congregational polity." Three hours of debate ranged over the "great theological and practical import" of the board's decision, and a motion was made to create a committee to study the issues involved, premised on the desire "that the conference remain a vital community of concerned Christians eager to act in a manner consistent with valid theological norms and our traditions of church polity." After that motion was defeated, the delegates approved "the intention and action" of the board of directors by a close vote, 269 for and 242 against. An event had occurred that would radically shape the life and ministry of the Massachusetts Conference of the United Church of Christ for the foreseeable future. Only with that business completed did the delegates turn to the matter of electing a new conference minister and president, who responded, "You have not suspended history to get me elected."

The following months found the United Church of Christ in Massachusetts straining at the seams. At the meeting on November 19, 1969, the directors—by a vote of 19 to 3—authorized the transfer of $250,000 early in 1970 to the Black Ecumenical Commission, as a first payment to implement their decision to give one million dollars to the B.E.C. That same day the board created a Dialogue Committee to explore with ministers and churches of the conference the full implications of the decision to make black empowerment and self-determination a paramount priority of the conference. A letter from the directors urged participation of the 190,000 United Churchmen of Massachusetts "in the agonizing decisions that will be necessary to make this gift from the conference assets." How agonizing, how painful, the choices would be is the story of the Massachusetts Conference in the year of our Lord 1970.

A staff member of the conference anticipated things to come when he wrote:

> When the church touches the life of the world on the vital issues confronting society hot conflict usually is generated.[9]

The climate of the conference was *charged*. Before their action of November 19, the Worcester Association asked the directors to slow down the implementation of their decision to facilitate "the consultative process wherein all the churches shall have the opportunity to discuss and act upon the empowerment of the

---

[9] Darrell Holland, *Pilgrim State News,* January 1970, a publication of the Massachusetts Conference of the United Church of Christ.

black community in the terms suggested by the Board of Directors." The Metropolitan Boston Association, on the other hand, passed a resolution commending the board, "for dealing with" the B.E.C. grant.

In a letter sent to all conference churches and ministers on November 28, 1969, one member of the board of directors submitted his resignation, in his belief

> that it was not the will or the intention of those who nominated me, nor those who elected me, to be a member of such a board having such all sweeping powers.

He urged others "to join me in repudiating" the actions of the board "in taking upon themselves the power of the conference." Then, he asked that all

> individuals and churches withhold their contributions paid to that conference through per capita dues and through Our Christian World Mission designated gifts.

A minister in the central part of the state charged that the directors' decision to transfer a substantial portion of conference assets to the Black Ecumenical Commission—supported by a narrow margin of conference delegates on October 18—was, in reality, funding "institutional segregation." He announced that he would

> cease, in every respect, to regard himself as a member of that conference

until it

> repudiates its policy of "interim separatism" and the funding of "institutional segregation."

Institutional survival of the churches of the conference caught, without their desire or consent, in the maelstrom of controversy was painfully expressed in a letter received in the conference office:

> As actions of the adjourned meeting and the Board of Directors are announced, I am more concerned than ever. Our members and large contributors read of these actions, and already we have statements that if any of the money from our church goes to pay for the Black Ecumenical Commission, their pledge is cancelled. We cannot survive as individual churches if this is to happen.

Such a statement must certainly be set against the background of the "black reparations" issue which has stirred hot feelings among church members in recent years, and the memory of those who witnessed the occupation of the speaker's platform by supporters of James Forman, when he spoke to the delegates of the General Synod of the United Church of Christ, convened in Boston in June 1969.

As the newly-elected conference minister and president, Avery Post was caught in the celebration and backlash of an event that was initiated prior to his presence on the Massachusetts scene. In a pastoral letter, December 5, 1969, he made his own stance known:

> I respect and honor the integrity of the struggle of the directors of the conference as they have sought to take initiatives to empower the black community through a grant from the accumulated mission funds of the conference.

He observed that "church bodies have a way of blessing priorities with rhetoric," then added that the board of directors of the Massachusetts Conference has made its choice to move "to the heart of the matter where issues are struggled out before God. I believe that the board, acting as a community of Christians, acted faithfully."

Recognizing the charge of the use or abuse of power, Dr. Post said:

> The board did not in some self-conscious way arrogate to itself the powers of the conference, but anguished over the responsibilities of God's church. . . . The action did not violate the trust between the conference and the church, but clearly tested it. And that is a nerve-racking business for all concerned.

He labeled the B.E.C. grant "providential" identifying black churchmen as "fellow Christians committed to the liberation of black people and the humanizing of society."

To the issue of black separatism and institutional segregation, he wrote:

> I do not regard black self-determination as ideological separatism, but a glorious and overdue chapter in the life of an oppressed and unbelievably patient people.

Regarding black empowerment, he asserted that

> the whole society is on the way to a quality of humanness and a sense of wholeness that black people alone have known deep in their hearts is not expressed by pursuing integration in an unrenewed

48

society. . . . The black man has a dream of a whole new people. I believe his dream is of God.

The financial crunch for the conference and the painful decisions that lay ahead were also realistically underscored. He termed the B.E.C. grant "a radical action" that would precipitate basic and fundamental changes in the life of the conference. His own confidence for the future was revealed through his affirmation that the crisis that is upon us:

> is not nearly as significant as the brimming awareness of mission and of missionary action that now begins to spread through the conference and its congregations.

He concluded:

> We live in a time of multiple and conflicting priorities. The church must be engaged with many of them.

The conference minister had now taken his own leadership position—with all the vulnerability that entailed. Neutrality, passivity, and caution were overcome by commitment and decisiveness as men and women throughout the conference struggled in a new way to discern and be faithful to the gospel of Jesus Christ. Christian discipleship, in the abstract, was now to be tested by responsiveness to a particular event and decision. Once again the Word was being made flesh.

Realization that the action within the United Church of Christ of Massachusetts had intruded into a larger arena came in a 400-word telegram on January 27, 1970, from Roy Wilkins, executive director of the National Association for the Advancement of Colored People. Dr. Wilkins charged that the decision to fund the B.E.C. encourages the "apostleship of black racism." This accusation by a veteran civil rights leader fanned the flames of controversy throughout the churches of the state, and, subsequently, the national leader of the NAACP became the focal point of conflict when the conference convened its annual meeting in the spring of 1970.

Immediate response was made to Roy Wilkins by inviting him to come to Boston on February 26, 1970, to discuss, with representatives of the conference, the issues of black self-determination. Illness made it impossible for Dr. Wilkins to accept, but the NAACP was ably represented by John Morsell, the assistant executive director. To speak in its behalf, the NAACP also brought to the February meeting, Stephen Gill Spottswood, bishop of the American Methodist Episcopal Zion Church, and Buell Gallagher, former president of the City College of New York. Bishop Spottswood, Chairman of the Board of the NAACP, dubbed white churchmen "gullible" in funding all black organizations like the B.E.C., and expressed amazement that no credibility had been given to the NAACP in reference to the grant of one million dollars. Dr. Gallagher placed himself "out of sympathy entirely with the misguided action of the Massachusetts Conference," and labeled as "blasphemy" any talk about black and white churches.

Supporters of the action by the Massachusetts Conference were equally vigorous and outspoken. Bishop James K. Matthews, of the United Methodist Church in New England, called the grant "an investment in justice and human dignity, pre-eminent concerns of our day." The Rt. Rev. Anson Phelps Stokes, Jr., retired bishop of the Episcopal Diocese of Massachusetts and president of the former Commission on Church and Race of the Massachusetts Council of Churches, defended the "rightness of the action," and argued that

> the emergence of distinctly black action in the church is correcting our insights, and there is much more correction to be done. Black demands have begun to help us see the issue from a black point of view.

Support for the B.E.C. grant from black leadership came through statements from Preston Williams of the Boston University School of Theology and Charles Cobb, the executive director of the national Commission for Racial Justice of the United Church of Christ. In addition the Rt. Rev. John M. Burgess, Episcopal bishop of Massachusetts, took issue with the NAACP in a letter to Avery D. Post on January 30, 1970, and wrote:

> Black self-determination and the strengthening of the black church is a goal fully consistent with the goal of integration and the Episcopal Church supports both. True and meaningful integration can become a reality through Black empowerment.
> I commend the United Church of Christ for its forthright action and clear demonstration of trust as evidenced by its grant to the Black Ecumenical Commission.

Hidden layers of pain, mistrust and subterfuge also surfaced at the February 26 meeting between representatives of the Massachusetts UCC and the NAACP. Dr. Post said to those assembled:

> I must say in full candor . . . that we were dismayed to have knowledge of the [Roy Wilkins'] telegram from the New York Times three hours before its arrival at my office in Boston on January 27. Clearly the NAACP has acted to give national breadth to the charge that the "racist separatist philosophy" had become the "mode of choice" in the action of the Massachusetts Conference to empower the black church through the Black Ecumenical Commission.

The January 27 telegram also indicated that the NAACP had been giving "advice and counsel" to opponents of the board's action since late November 1969.

Within the Massachusetts Conference the position of the dissenters to the decision of the directors was made clear in a letter of January 2, 1970, sent to all churches and ministers and signed by seven ministers and one layman. The letter charged that the grant has

> shattered the bond of confidence and trust that is so vitally needed between the local church and the state conference.

The letter advocated diverting funds from the conference, not "as a punitive proposal, but rather as the only way in which we can fulfill our responsibility of Christian stewardship."

During this same period 10 members of the Youth Council of the Massachusetts United Church of Christ issued a statement identifying the grant as a "follow through with deeds rather than words alone." They expressed that they were

> impressed by this courageous attempt by the conference to respond to one of the most pressing needs of our time, the crisis of racial inequality and powerlessness.

The youth cited the action as

> an excellent educational opportunity for our churches and youth to discuss the implications of the grant and the larger issue of black-white relations. . . . Dialogue on the meaning of this grant may help more of us to confront this issue, instead of avoiding it.

This insight underscores what has long been recognized by many in the church that Christian education designed to change one's commitments and life-style takes place only in relationship to specific events, not in the abstract. Information about Christianity may be transmitted in a detached manner, but education that alters human behavior occurs in the hot matrix of action and particularity.

The hot matrix, created by the decision to give one million

dollars of conference assets to the Black Ecumenical Commission, continued unabated in the early months of 1970 and escalated as the June annual meeting approached. The 25-man dialogue committee moved among the churches to fulfill its assigned responsibility:

> To confront the local church with its mission, and to engage the church in a discussion of the role of the church as a change agent in society.

The directors of the conference came together for meetings of six to eight hours duration, the conference staff labored day and night, while ministers and churches of the conference aligned themselves across the whole spectrum of responses generated by the issues that clustered around the grant.

Three foci developed:

(1) A sharp decline in 1969 in giving by conference churches to Our Christian World Mission, the financial support structure of the conference and national instrumentalities, continued in 1970. Was the B.E.C. grant the reason, or were there other factors? The financial attrition being experienced by all denominations indicated that many factors were at work influencing financial contributions by all churches.

(2) By-law changes to regulate the life of the conference were being drafted that included drastic reductions in the power of the Board of Directors.

(3) A March 10 letter, signed by 75 conference ministers requested the directors to invite Roy Wilkins to present his views in opposing the B.E.C. grant at the annual meeting, June 5–6, 1970.

The issue of the Wilkins' invitation moved to the center of attention in the days immediately preceding the annual meeting.

The directors took the position that Dr. Wilkins—though a well-known and respected civil rights leader—was only one voice speaking for the black community, who espoused a position that did not represent many other national black leaders. Inquiry was made as to the availability of other black leaders to speak to the annual meeting of the conference, and when they declined to enter this particular arena of hot debate and controversy, the board of directors determined not to extend an invitation to Roy Wilkins. However the matter did not stop there: it only established the lines for the initial confrontation at the annual meeting—through which those who took positions on the B.E.C. grant would test their strength.

The depth of feelings that was the environment for conference business was symbolized by the decision of Bishop Stephen Gill Spottswood to withdraw as a con-celebrant in the ecumenical service of Holy Communion for the installation of Avery D. Post as minister and president of the Massachusetts Conference of the United Church of Christ. In a June 2 telegram, Bishop Spottswood gave voice to his own particular anguish:

> With deep regret and after carefully weighing the alternatives, I have concluded that I must decline your invitation to participate in your installation. . . . Our fundamental disagreement regarding your conference's grant to the Black Ecumenical Commission, which I am certain only serves the divisive purposes of those seeking two societies in America, was well known when the invitation was issued. . . .
>
> Now the decision of your Board of Directors against making it possible for the delegates to hear Roy Wilkins, executive director of the NAACP, over whose highest governing body I preside, would seem to seal the pages of further debate. As a senior bishop in a black church founded in protest against racial exclusion, I cannot in conscience allow even the suggestion of my acquiescence in policies which, however well-meaning, are a rebuff to the principles which the NAACP has served and continues to serve so effectively.

On June 3, Dr. Post replied:

> We feel pain at your decision to withdraw from the con-celebrated service of Holy Communion. . . . We affirm again our belief that the Black Ecumenical Commission is an agent of the church and that it promotes black self determination and black empowerment and racial justice.

As the conference annual meeting opened for business on June 5, the 1,000 delegates and visitors were immediately confronted with a motion to alter the suggested agenda and extend an invitation to Dr. Wilkins to address the conference. His availability had already been established by advocates for his presence. After heated debate the motion to invite the noted civil rights leader was defeated 488 to 282—thus ending the intervention of Roy Wilkins and the NAACP in the B.E.C. grant issue of the Massachusetts Conference. A short time later the delegates went on to affirm their support for the grant to the Black Ecumenical Commission by a vote of 611 for and 194 against—marking a dramatic shift of support for the board action since the recessed meeting of October 1969.

Despite the unusually heavy commitment of time and emotional energy to the issue of funding the B.E.C., delegates to the annual meeting also responded forthrightly to other critical issues on the world's agenda and voted an allocation of $5,350 of conference funds to establish draft counseling centers in strategically located churches throughout the commonwealth and an additional $5,000 for the National Council of Churches emergency ministry to draft-age emigrants in Canada.[10] That action was coupled with a vote placing the conference "on record as condemning the invasion of Cambodia by the U.S. and its Allies," and called "for withdrawal of all U.S. military personnel from Indochina by a stated date." The march of historical events in the arenas of race and peace required and received priority action. Whatever one's position on particular issues, no delegate left the June 1970 meeting of the Massachusetts Conference of the United Church of Christ without being aware that the conference and its churches, ministers and laymen were alive and active in a new way.

That spirit and vitality continued unabated in subsequent months as the conference grappled with issues of priorities, budgets, and proposed bylaw changes. The churches and ministers were prepared to heed the warning of their elected leader of the danger that "churches will be non-revolutionary in these revolutionary times." For additional data of the pain and power that permeate the Christian church in the latter third of the twentieth century I turn attention to the midwest.

THE NEBRASKA STORY

"God damn the churches—who gives a damn about the church? —burn them all down." Those words, attributed to a resource leader of a Youth Leadership Conference for the United Churches of Christ of Nebraska, are the opening sentence of a letter dated September 12, 1969, and sent to ministers and many lay members of those churches. It was signed by a minister serving one of the conference churches, a member of the conference board of directors, and a woman active in her church. The letter provides the context to examine another conference in conflict. The story behind it and the reactions and results brought forth

---

[10] The Annual Meeting of the Nebraska Conference of the United Church of Christ, convened in Lincoln, April 17-19, 1970, also "commended and thanked the Canadian Council of Churches for providing pastoral care to the draft-age Americans in Canada," and urged "its churches to show their concern for these men, through voluntary contributions of money and in other appropriate ways." No doubt many church bodies have taken similar actions.

by the circulation of the letter, reveal the church of Christ undergoing "baptism by fire." What can we learn? What must we do to equip ministers and churches to survive those experiences that try men's souls, lacerate their spirits and divide the community of faith?

It is a story of an event that constellated many long standing resentments and feelings of dissatisfaction among members of Nebraska UCC churches. In a society of rapid change; uncertainty, bewilderment and anxiety build up to an explosive pressure, waiting only for some occasion to release the eruption. A youth conference provided that outlet for churches of the Nebraska Conference. By examining this particular experience, it is possible to anticipate the leadership needs of many churches caught in the crunch.

From August 10-16, 1969, a Youth Leadership Conference was held on the campus of Doane College sponsored by the Nebraska Conference of the United Church of Christ and the Synod of Nebraska of the United Presbyterian Church, U.S.A. Attending were 32 teenagers—ranging from the 9th through the 12th grades. In addition there were 10 adults—including the UCC state minister of education, Donald A. Gall, and Russell F. Mertz, minister of a conference church, who served as camp director. The theme of the Leadership Conference was publicized in advance: "Give a Damn—A Look at Love"—based on the popular youth record by Spanky and Our Gang, "Give a Damn for Your Fellowman." Advance publicity indicated that this issue would be developed through "experiences in sensitivity training and communication skills"—though the meaning of that was not spelled out—and a series of films on "some of the burning issues of our day." Resource leaders would include "exciting and provocative personalities":

> Ralph Moore:
>> Former national staff member of the United Church of Christ Youth Ministry, who has worked with Black Power and militant student groups;
> Arkie King:
>> Former seminary student from Boston, acquainted with the hippie community of that city;
> Phil Medcalf:
>> A student at the University of Nebraska and former member of Students for a Democratic Society (SDS);
> Josephine Scott:
>> Representing the UCC Stewardship Council, and a person who has been actively involved in civil rights demonstrations.

As the conference got underway, the director called the adults together the first afternoon to give them the following instructions:

> I told the adult participants that they were to simply be adult participants; that they had no leadership responsibilities except to be with the youth, listen, to comment as they wished. . . . I instructed the resource persons to be themselves.
>
> During the course of that meeting, it was suggested that if we really wanted to find out what it meant to love in terms of what we planned, that all persons at the Conference should have equal responsibility for what happened each day. This was discussed, and finally agreed upon.

Thus, in the opening hours, the adults determined that they would launch into the week's events without structure or rules being imposed by them upon the teenagers. They would run the risk of letting each one be himself, thereby making the collective decision-making process the learning experience. In the words of the director:

> It required that the leaders and other adults step out of their role as leaders or as "authority figures" if all were, in fact, to experience responsibility for what was done during the week.

In retrospect he noted:

> It became very apparent that this was very frustrating at first. The youth, not used to this, were uneasy; the adults, equally not accustomed to this, were also frustrated. Yet, we did begin to see decisions being made and groups meeting to discuss and do things pertinent to our theme.

For most teenage and adult participants the week's experiences were indeed something new and different. Allowed the freedom to be—unfettered and uninhibited by the decision to remove the usual structures and rules—they began to discover themselves and one another in a new and explosive way. The normal propriety in the use of language gave way to a more "gutsy vocabulary" and the inhibitions that normally surround discussions of God, church, parents, country, war and peace, racism, and school gave way to an honest expression of real feelings and the search for one's own convictions about life's basic issues, *whether they conformed to conventional norms or not*. In a church setting—everything was up for grabs—and truth had to stand on its own two feet without the usual props of structure or rules or imposed doctrinal orthodoxy. It was a heady wine, for which most institutions are ill prepared, and most adult leaders are unwilling to risk. In the light of subsequent events it is clear that much more preparation should have been given in the program design of the youth conference, especially to the adults who had been asked to participate. Purpose and intent should have been clearly delineated by the program planners, for freedom and openness in a group setting require more preparation than a conference structured along the usual lines of authority.

Soon after the Leadership Youth Conference had concluded, one of the adult participants held a lengthy meeting with John Newman, chairman of the board of directors of the Nebraska Conference of the UCC, to express her grave concern over the nature of the youth conference and her negative reactions to it. Recognizing the gravity of the concerns expressed to him, Mr. Newman requested that the Commission on Educational Ministries determine a means to evaluate the youth conference and make a full report to the board of directors of the Nebraska Conference of the UCC at their September meeting. The commission set Saturday, September 13, as the date for a "hearing" at which all interested parties would be invited to express their concerns and opinions. Human passions did not wait for due process, however.

Early in the same week that had been set for the hearing a member of the conference directors was shown a letter by an adult participant at the youth conference. The letter contained serious charges regarding the personal, moral conduct of those who shared in the experiences at Doane College the week of August 10-16. Verbal assurances were given that nothing would be done with the letter until after the hearing which had been set for Saturday of that week. However, on Saturday morning, September 13, the minister of First-Plymouth Church, Lincoln, had a copy of the letter, which he showed to the Conference Minister, Scott S. Libbey. That same night, at a reception in his honor, Senator Roman Hruska of Nebraska made reference to the troubles of the Nebraska Conference of the United Church of Christ, the details of which he had received in a letter that had been mailed to him. Within hours the members of the board of directors and the staff of the UCC Nebraska Conference realized that prior to the hearing that had been set to review the youth conference, a five-page document, containing very serious charges, had been distributed to a wide mailing list. Most of the letters—in a plain envelope without a return address—were postmarked in Lincoln, Saturday A.M., September 13, the morning of the hearing. In the immediate days that followed, the staff and directors learned that the letter, containing the charges, was in the hands of every UCC minister in Nebraska, many lay members of the churches, the newspapers, local and state police, the F.B.I., as well as Nebraska's Congressmen and Senators.

The letter made the most serious allegations as to what had occurred at the Youth Leadership Conference:

> All week the resource people advocated anti-church, anti-parent, anti-establishment, anti-American sentiments and activities. We were shown underground movies always portraying police brutality and anti-Americanism, i.e., showing draft-card burnings, demonstrations, riots, the Chicago Democratic Convention riots, the march on the Pentagon, Dr. Benjamin Spock, and Rev. Coffin from Yale demonstrating, etc. always from the biased viewpoint of the demonstrators.
>
> The President of the College has requested that the Youth Leadership Conference not be held at Doane again. . . .
>
> We were told that one of the resource leaders sent two camper boys in the country to hunt marijuana for him. . . .
>
> We understood the person from the UCC National Stewardship Council to advocate evading the draft by burning draft cards, by taking LSD to avoid being drafted, and by failure to register for the draft. She also advocated burning down "Whitey's" buildings and apartments as they aren't good for anything anyhow.
>
> One resource person from the UCC National Youth Ministry Board told the group that in his opinion, "Cuba is wonderful; that will be our third world; and that Fidel is great."
>
> It appeared to us that there was much consumption of alcoholic beverages by many of the adult participants, as well as campers, both on campus and off campus.

Regarding sensitivity experiences the letter said:

> Many specialists in the field of psychiatry recognize self-criticism (or sensitivity training or finding oneself) to be an integral part of the brain-washing technique used so destructively by the Chinese communists on our military in Korea. A recent radio program on KOA, Denver, inferred that sensitivity training was highly sex-oriented.

The letter sent to the churches charged gross "use of vulgar language" condoned as " 'feeling' words straight from the 'gut' " and added the following accusation:

> Included in their tactics at Conference were: a "feel-in" where participants shut their eyes and hugged, kissed and felt each other (boy-boy, girl-girl, boy-girl). . . . Many of the boys and girls as well as some resource leaders slept together either out in a field or in the dormitory lounge or flopped down on unassigned mattresses in the dormitory.

A bomb had burst that would penetrate every segment of the Nebraska Conference of the United Church of Christ. It was a time that would test the spirits, for some were destined to lose their jobs, while others lost their innocence, and a few surrendered their integrity.

After receiving a full report from the executive committee of the Commission on Educational Ministries following their "hearing" on September 13, the board of directors of the UCC Nebraska Conference held a news conference on September 19 to make public their findings and conclusions regarding the Leadership Youth Conference.

The report expressed deep regret that the letter containing such serious allegations had been widely circulated before the Commission on Educational Ministries or the board of directors had the opportunity to evaluate and act, especially inasmuch as although some statements in the letter were substantiated, many were not.

In its evaluation the board discovered an inadequate clarification of goals, standards, and expectations by those who had planned the Leadership Youth Conference believing

> that in this event the Conference Director and the Minister of Christian Education of the State Conference abrogated the special leadership responsibility which we believe was theirs. The Board believes that the adult leadership of the conference became so involved in the process of the conference and its potential meaning that they were not able to objectify the meaning of the conference and its implications for the total life of our churches.

In its findings the board also reported that the youth conference resource leaders did not reflect a balance consistent with the wide spectrum represented by the churches, and "that, in the future, we must use greater care in securing competent leadership which will reflect a greater balance of backgrounds and programming." Recognizing the inherent dangers of employing an educational design that is new and not understood by those invited to participate, the board stressed that in the future

> there should be a clear interpretation of purposes and procedures made to potential participants, both youth and adult, before a Conference is held. Such advance interpretation should be available to both potential participants and their families.

The cost of surprise is one of the hard lessons of the Nebraska story. Advance interpretation of the educational design could have gained prior consent by all participants, or prompted those who did not understand or agree to withdraw voluntarily and not be placed in an embarrassing or hostile environment.

Responding to the more serious moral charges the board reached the following conclusions:

> Obscenities and vulgarities as used at the Youth Leadership Conference are unnecessary and inappropriate. [The Board] does not believe that the use of such language shocks people into caring. It further agrees that we cannot condone or permit the use of alcohol, drugs or immoral sexual activities. In making this statement the Board wishes to emphasize that it found no evidence that immoral sexual activities took place at this conference, or that drugs were used or were in any way on the premises at the time of this conference.

The board also recognized the embarrassment caused to Doane College and concurred "that this conference could have been more responsible as a tenant at Doane College and that in the future, in accord with the desire of the college, the college should be involved in the planning process and execution of the conference."

Having listed the inadequacies and failures cited above, for which the board of directors and the Nebraska Conference staff felt ultimately responsible, the report of the board at their September 19 news conference then reflected the reactions of the youth participants who attended the leadership conference that had caused such a stir among the UCC Nebraska churches. They reported that "20 of the 23 young people who had sent in evaluations of the meeting affirmed that the Youth Leadership Conference was extremely meaningful and significant and aided in their Christian growth." They added:

> The Board confesses its incompetency to always bridge the gap between the generations and understand fully the ways in which youth appropriate the Faith and grow in it. We can only report that many of the young people did witness to such growth and we delight in that.

While being compelled by circumstances to focus upon the youth conference, the board, in its public report, also acknowledged the larger issue:

> The Board recognizes that the problem of division is larger than the specific incident of the Youth Leadership Conference. In many ways this has been the spark which has ignited a lot of problems that have been around for a long time and threatens to become a conflagration.
>
> The Board of Directors recognizes that many of the people in our

churches, both laymen and ministers, have felt a sense of alienation from much of the direction of the Conference, the denomination and the wider church, for sometime. It further recognizes that this problem is not one which is solely resident in the United Church of Christ, but in fact is a problem that runs through all of American Christianity in our day. At almost every turn in our contemporary history there seems to be a threat which would rend asunder the Body of Christ.

The board's report sets this rupture in the context of the current struggle to identify the role of the church in contemporary society—a debate with which every reader of this book can identify.

In many ways this is brought into being as dedicated Christian people decide to seek to struggle with the whole question as to how the church is most relevant and faithful in our world. The church moves today, when it moves at all, without the unanimity of its members.

Further, there are increasing evidences of rejection in many of our churches of a style of leadership at the helm of our organized church life.

But the potential for division and threat of polarization are very real problems. As many would seek to pull us back from an activist style of ministry that is contemporary in its language, forms and symbols—many others would see this as the only hope for the renewal of the church.

The Youth Leadership Conference did not cause the division of the church, but has instead been the instance in which that division has become most apparent to us.

It was in that larger context that the board received and accepted at its meeting on September 18, a letter of resignation from Donald A. Gall, minister of Christian education of the Nebraska Conference. Mr. Gall's letter further illuminates the deeper crisis confronting the church:

Never before in the history of the church has it been more important for the church to be united in its ministry and mission to the world than it is today. Yet, even now, the fellowship of our church is being threatened from within because of the alleged happenings at a recent youth conference for which I was responsible as the Conference Minister of Christian Education.

This board, through the office of its chairman, requested that a process of evaluation be established by the Commission on Education Ministries in order to ascertain the facts and to present their findings at the time of this meeting. Three persons, who were present at the youth conference and who objected to what happened there, were invited to be a part of the evaluation process and to voice concerns at that time. Those people chose to circumvent this procedure and to make their allegations known to a wide number of persons throughout this conference through the use of a letter, a document which also found its way into the hands of newsmen and government officials. That many of their allegations were not and could not be substantiated did not deter them from their crusade to "save the church from destruction," nor has it tempered many individuals within the church in their desire to judge and condemn me without benefit of all the facts.

This board is now faced with the awesome task of dealing constructively with a fellowship of churches that is at this moment torn by controversy and the threat of disintegration, when instead it should be strongly united behind a common ministry to the world. I deeply regret the part that I have played which has brought the state of our church to this sad and sorry condition.

As the Conference Minister of Christian Education, I have tried to be faithful to all of the responsibilities of my ministry. That I have made mistakes during these past five years, or that I have not always exercised the best judgment, I will not deny. But I cannot and will not agree with those who say that I love not the church or those to whom I have ministered, and that because of my "unorthodox" manners I have deliberately tried to "corrupt" and lead the youth of this conference astray.

Yet the controversy with which you must deal has centered around me and the position I hold on the conference staff. I am convinced that many of our members, together with an apparently growing number of churches, no longer have confidence in my ability or desire to minister to their needs. I am also convinced that my continued presence as a member of this conference Staff can no longer serve the best interests of this conference.

It is therefore with deep regret, but with concern for the unity and strength of this conference, that I hereby submit my resignation as Conference Minister of Christian Education, effective December 31, 1969.

Respectfully submitted,

Donald A. Gall

With deep regret the directors accepted the resignation "because it cannot find it within itself to attempt to persuade a man to minister in a situation devoid of trust." Removed from the *heat of the moment* these questions are appropriate to ask: Should Mr. Gall have resigned under duress? Should the board have tried to persuade him to reconsider and make his decision in quieter moments? Does the church have no alternative but to sacrifice its faithful servants when they are crucified by its own members?

The action of a few also claimed another victim. In a letter dated September 28, 1969, Russell F. Mertz, who had served as Director of the Youth Conference, submitted his letter of resignation to the congregations of St. Luke's and Gruetli United Churches of Christ, whom he had served as their pastor.

The past few weeks have caused a mighty burden to fall upon all of us who are involved in the life of our congregations.

Stemming from allegations mailed to a small number of persons within our congregations, these weeks have been fraught with tension, misunderstanding, mistrust, and anguish.

Although responsible bodies of churchmen—both lay and clergy —have dispelled many of the charges which were printed in this letter signed by three persons outside our congregations, little can be done to overcome the doubt and distrust that I sense now prevails in these congregations toward me.

During my pastorate here, I feel much has been done to alert both congregations to what it means to be the church—that is, to be those who are called by the Lord of the church to accept, among other things, the cost and joy of discipleship. And, I do not regret the stance I have taken nor the particular style of leadership I have lived.

I do regret that an atmosphere of openness and trust has not prevailed to the extent that all could feel free to share with me their feelings of frustration, anger, uncertainty, doubt, as well as those of joy, hope, and possibility. And, perhaps, I was partly responsible for that failure.

However, in light of the current situation confronting us, it has become abundantly clear to me that I could not now really deal effectively with the people of our congregations. I am also convinced that to remain here indefinitely would not permit all persons in these congregations to deal with me and with each other openly, honestly, and positively for the sake of the church in these communities.

I have constantly advocated that all we do we do for the sake of others and on behalf of the Lord of history. It is with this in mind that I seek from you, the members of these congregations, an affirmation of a decision I have made.

I respectfully request your affirmation of my desire to terminate my relationship with you effective December 31, 1969.

Respectfully submitted,

Russell F. Mertz

The mistrust, pain, and hurt—centered upon the Youth Leadership Conference, but more deeply rooted in the life of the churches—were personally wounding the lives of Christian men and women and their families. It was in the midst of this cauldron of agony that the directors held their press conference, which was soon followed by intense and passionate conversations at the fall Association meetings of the Nebraska Conference, scheduled the weekend of September 21-24 to hear reports of the delegates to the Seventh General Synod. The meetings were held, with unprecedented attendance, but the agenda was radically changed. The members of the churches of the conference were in communication with one another in a new and painful way.

In the perspective of the two years that have passed since the youth conference was held on the Doane College campus in August 1969, some observations are pertinent.

1. The evidence sustains the board's insight that the issue was much broader than one youth conference. That was the vehicle to surface buried resentments and dissatisfactions. The dilemmas facing church leaders under such circumstances are revealed in the following communication sent to the directors:

November 2, 1969

Mr. John W. Newman, Chairman, Board of Directors
Nebraska Conference United Church of Christ
2055 E Street, Lincoln, Nebraska 68510

Dear Mr. Newman:

I am writing to you, the Chairman of the Board of Directors, because of a personal concern for the welfare of the United Church of Christ in Nebraska and for the futures of two individuals, the Rev. Russell Mertz and the Rev. Donald A. Gall. The Church's state structure and these two men have suffered through an unjust series of events which has led not only to their resignations, but also to an aura of distrust which now surrounds them and the Church. This aura encompasses and will continue to encompass these individuals and others who share their convictions, as well as the whole state structure of our church, unless the Board of Directors takes a new, more specific action with regard to the signers and backers of the now famous "trinitarian" letter.

In my opinion, this letter, which I have skimmed with dismay, was a prime example of more to come from a giant "iceberg" of discontent and misunderstanding in the local churches. The fall Association meetings became open forums for emotional outpourings of many concerns. Certainly these concerns should be voiced and every effort made to heal misunderstandings, but if more individuals act as irresponsibly and unethically as did the authors of the above-mentioned letter, I feel the Board will have to take some of the blame for the consequences. The individual signers and those who backed their actions should have been severely reprimanded for the unethical act of mailing the letter before the hearing and should have been taken to court for slander if necessary in order to restore at least to some degree the trust in the characters of Russ Mertz and Don Gall. Instead the Board by its middle-of-the-road position has given license for more of the same type of vicious approaches to the airing of emotionally-based concerns.

I am sickened by the suffering I know these men, their families, and friends have undergone because of a few persons, but I am sickened even more by the inability of the Church's structure to function effectively behind Russ Mertz and Don Gall against this kind of malicious attack.

Sincerely,

Jane Kluck
(Mrs. Fred Kluck, Jr.)
3535 South 40 Street
Lincoln, Nebr. 68506

Member: Federated Church
Columbus, Nebr.

For the most part, the church has not yet learned how to lance its own infections in a way that allows differences and conflicts to be expressed naturally and freely in an atmosphere of toleration and love. By burying its problems—in the false assumption that "nice people" don't express themselves openly and honestly for fear of hurting one another—the church invites disaster and chaos in the aftermath of a volcanic explosion that will occur when the pressure becomes intolerable.

2. The differences in response of the youth and adults point up the separation that exists among older and younger church members, which will have a radical effect upon the church of the future unless the gap is closed. Another letter illuminates what is at stake for the church:

> Moritorium Day, 1969
> Trinity College
> P. O. Box 558
> Hartford, Connecticut
> 06106
>
> To the members of the Board of Directors of the Nebraska Conference of the UCC,
>
> My name is Bob Hurst. I served for three years on the Nebraska Youth Ministry Board of the UCC, and I am currently a member of the Council for Christian Social Action of the UCC.
>
> Though I have had to observe the proceedings concerning the Doane Conference from afar, I have been piecing together a story of what has happened, drawing upon the Board's report, letters from young people at the Conference, and personal knowledge gathered from three years experience in the Nebraska Youth Ministry. The story which unfolds before me I do not like! I would like to share with you my reaction to your report. My words are angry, and I assume that my thoughts will reflect a generation gap so large, that you may not be able to see over to my side of the chasm. I at least ask you to read on, because the church must come to some accommodation with the young voices within her, or there will be no church in 30 years, and I perhaps more than you wish to preserve the church which we both love, but not in formaldehyde.
>
> In your report you mention, "the Commission should find high on its agenda of responsibilities the clarification of goals, standards, and expectations under which people operate at such conferences." I ask you, how many young people are on the Commission on Educational Ministries? I assert that young people have the responsibility for defining their own goals and destinies and not a church board comprised predominately of persons who could not be classified as young people. The Youth Ministry Board and the Youth Program of the church have operated apart from the rest of the church, because they have been excluded from meaningful participation in the church.
>
> How many churches still require that an individual be 21 before he can vote in his local church? Does the composition of the Annual Conference Meeting reflect the number of young people that are in

the church? How many young people sit on the Board of Directors of the Nebraska Conference, or the Commission on Educational Ministries? The General Synod of the UCC adopted a resolution asking that all church governing boards should include at least 20% participation from young people. How well has the Nebraska Conference measured up to these goals? How long does the Board of Directors expect young people to accept adult censorship, while the youth are systematically excluded from church office and policy making?

How many adult groups have asked for youth leadership and supervision, yet the Board wishes to cram adult opinions and censorship down the throats of young people. Again systematically the church refuses to recognize youth leadership and does not try to understand or support that leadership. Instead more adults with assuredly conservative backgrounds must be sent as non-involved censors to future gatherings of youth. (My understanding of the Board's report may be totally out in left field, but your recommendations seem suppressive, and they guarantee no means by which the youth can say no to adult censorship.)

Your comments about obscenity demonstrate the church's occupancy of the Ivory Tower. If our church leaders were to descend to the world of reality, where young people are currently engaged in battles on the peace front, sitting in the hunger trenches, and participating in the guerilla warfare of race relations, they would find that the only vulgar words are words like: NIGGER, DEFOLIATION, NAPALM, PACIFICATION, ABM, MIRV, ICBM, PIT. These are the true obscene words of our day, because they represent man's effort at senseless self-destruction.

Though my letter may reflect a hopefully bridgeable gap, I must place the burden of trust and responsibility for future efforts of reconciliation between youth and adults upon the shoulders of the Board of Directors of the Nebraska Conference of the UCC. May I give some suggestions of how I think that this needed reconciliation might come about. First, the Board of Directors should give a call for a youth convention to meet in December (youth 15-30). Such a convention should be comprised of representatives from youth groups throughout the state, college students representing both campuses in Nebraska and those students who maintain church membership within the state but go out of state to school, and young adults (college graduates to age thirty). Such a gathering should have the power to: draft resolutions to be sent to the Annual Conference Meeting, elect a number of delegates to the Annual Conference Meeting which would represent a minimum of 20% of the entire number of delegates at Annual Conference Meeting, nominate at least 20% of the seats of all Boards, Commissions and Councils of the Conference.

If the Board of Directors were to institute such reforms, then the young people of the state could meaningfully talk to the Board about its report and recommendations for conference youth programs. If the Board is interested in these recommendations, they should get in touch with Sara Ashby, 803 Sandoz, 820 North 17th, Lincoln, Nebraska 68508.

If this letter is transmitted to you, I would like to thank Rev. Scott Libbey, to whom I have entrusted my message.

Sincerely,

Bob Hurst

The long-range impact—as seen by parents—upon the youth who shared in the experience on the Doane College campus in August 1969 is also revealing. Parents interviewed in the spring of 1971 were unanimous in their appraisal of the positive effects. They confessed they would have been very anxious if they had known the format of the Youth Conference in advance, but attested to the affirmative impact upon their children. The comment of one parent was typical:

> It was one of the most fruitful experiences for my daughter that she has ever had. She was shy and self-depreciating, and it got her out of her shell. It changed her behavior.

3. A sensitive area for the directors of the Nebraska Conference was their feelings of an inadequate supportive role from the national denominational leadership of the United Church of Christ. A national staff person had participated in the youth conference and the Nebraska Conference minister, Scott S. Libbey, had formerly been on the staff of the Division of Christian Education of the denomination. A telephone call or two did occur and the sense of separation and aloneness may reflect the subjective feelings of the directors, but something more was expected. When no adequate response was received, one director wrote, "Your silence is deafening." When a response did come in January 1970, it seemed to the directors both defensive and late. It is an object lesson in the required sensitivities that must be developed within a caring, supportive community. The urgency of learning how to care for one another within the Christian fellowship is commensurate with the pressures and pain that are being experienced.

The questions are: How can the various instrumentalities of the church be supportive of one another? How can a conference assist a local church and its leadership in times of crisis? How can a national structure be helpful to a conference? The autonomy of congregational polity makes those questions difficult to answer. But they are critical and demand more attention. When the crisis comes, it is accompanied by a severe sense of loneliness and isolation. How one church received effective help will be reviewed in a later chapter. One director of the Nebraska Conference was quite realistic when he said, "We should have asked for the help we needed."

4. The financial health of the Nebraska Conference is another measurement of the impact and effect of crisis upon the church.

In September 1969—when the crisis-producing letter was circulated—conference receipts were down 10% from the previous year. By December 31, 1969, the financial loss, in comparison to 1968, was only 5%. In 1970 the Conference sustained an additional 2.25% reduction compared to 1969. This compares favorably however to other conferences of the United Church of Christ—with or without crisis. In 1971 financial pledges from conference churches indicate the dollar income will again rise. From the perspective of the directors the spirit and vitality of the conference are excellent. They report "new awareness" of the role of the church and "new involvement."

The Nebraska story is another indication that the crunch being experienced by the church today is exceedingly painful—especially for those in the most vulnerable positions—but is also the matrix of growth and learning. It is a story that illuminates the importance of leadership training and organizational development that are the foci of later chapters. Before turning to those critical issues however, attention will first be directed to the United Church of Christ in its national, denomination expression.

THE UNITED CHURCH OF CHRIST

Ferment and turmoil within the church are not localized. Upheaval and tension are not peculiar to any denomination; they bubble through every area of the church's life. Conflict and change are marks of the church in the latter half of the twentieth century. The pain and fragmentation, the potential and the hope of the church, in its national, denominational expression, are symbolized by the Seventh General Synod of the United Church of Christ, which convened in Boston, Massachusetts, June 25—July 2, 1969. The issues facing the church were multiple. The focal points to test those issues were two: the election of a new president for the United Church and the participation of James Forman of Black Manifesto fame.

Well in advance of Synod it was known that the choice for president of the official Nominating Committee was Robert V. Moss, Jr., president of Lancaster Theological Seminary. Black churchmen put forth their candidate—Arthur D. Gray, minister of the Congregational Church of Park Manor, Chicago, Illinois. A third selection for the office of president, Paul E. Gibbons, a chaplain at Cornell University, was proposed by United Churchmen for Change—an ad hoc group of national staff, local church ministers and laity that was formed in March 1969. Their purpose in entering the ecclesiastical, electoral process was to provide a platform to raise urgent issues that many felt were being neglected by the propensity of the Synod to carry on "business as usual" in a revolutionary time. An electoral contest that focussed on principles and issues—thereby challenging established ecclesiastical policy and procedures—was both a new and disturbing phenomenon for many delegates and church officers at the Seventh General Synod. However, a precedent had been set by the Sixth General Synod of 1967, when the nominating committee's recommendation for Church Secretary was defeated by a black candidate. As in every other segment of society good taste and propriety—which often allow entrenched authority and power to remain unchallenged and undisturbed—were giving way to struggle and conflict within the church over issues that sharply divided church members and leaders. United Churchmen for Change defined its own position in the following platform:

> In the name of the new humanity inaugurated in Jesus Christ, we shall press the United Church of Christ to move:
>
> 1) beyond middle-class prudence toward risking our total institutional life and resources in resistance to all forms of corporate violence, and in support of the liberation of the blacks, the poor, the powerless, and the young;
>
> 2) beyond arguing about re-structuring and merging the churches toward a flexible ecumenism embracing all groups and persons working to create a just society;
>
> 3) beyond a church politics that has disinherited the future toward empowering the young at all levels of church decision-making;
>
> 4) beyond residential ministries to the individual toward issue-oriented ministries functioning at all levels of American society.[11]

Measured by its success in electoral politics, United Churchmen for Change hardly created a ripple at the Seventh General Synod. The candidate of the nominating committee won decisively: 437 votes for Robert V. Moss, Jr.; 241 for Arthur D. Gray; and 41 for Paul E. Gibbons. However, set in the midst of the fermentation that made change inevitable—soon or late—the various caucuses that surfaced at the General Synod in Boston (black, youth, and United Churchmen for Change) had a signif-

---

[11] From a brochure distributed by Paul Gibbons to the delegates of the Seventh General Synod of the United Church of Christ.

icant and healthy effect, and presaged what was to come for the United Church of Christ.

During the first day of business the decorum of Synod was shattered and the anger and frustration of some delegates broke into the open. The background was the action taken by the directors of the Board of World Ministries in joining in a restraining order against the National Black Economic Conference, following their occupancy of offices at the Interchurch Center, 475 Riverside Drive, New York City. The presence of James Forman, who had been invited to address the Synod delegates, made the issue all the more sensitive. Just how sensitive was soon apparent when a group of delegates and visitors occupied the stage to demand that the scheduled agenda be set aside in order that the Synod might respond to the black agenda—an item to which the church has been giving lip service for many years, but without substance. Good manners—and the scheduled address by the president of the church, Ben M. Herbster—were swept aside by the anger and pain of church members. Crunch at the highest levels of operation of the United Church of Christ was now a public reality.

It was announced that the Business Committee intended action relating to having the Board of World Ministries withdraw its name from the restraining order against the National Black Economic Conference. Immediately a motion was approved that the Synod recess until the Business Committee was ready to report. Delegates were unwilling to proceed with the stated agenda until this priority issue was resolved. With feelings at a high pitch, the Business Committee reported in the late afternoon and recommended that the Board for World Ministries withdraw from its participation in the restraining order. For all present there was an acute awareness that the events of the world had impinged upon the church at work in a painful way. It was only the beginning, though attention that would be given to other issues was less visible and volatile by comparison.

Those associated with United Churchmen for Change pressed for action on three fronts:

1. A use of church investments that would be more responsive to critical social needs.
2. More equitable age representation among delegates to future Synod meetings, and among those who would serve on boards and committees that would formulate church policy.
3. The development of resources and a program that would insure action at the grassroots level of the church.

The issue of church investments was especially sensitive for those responsible for the portfolio management of the Board for Homeland Ministries, the Board for World Ministries and the Pension Board. For the Synod delegates the issue was inevitably associated with the Black Manifesto and the demand for reparations from the church. Some associated with the Pension Board felt that an effort was being made to undercut their legal responsibility to those who were dependent upon annuity payments in the latter years of their life. In fact, however, the question was never one of legal responsibilities and moral obligations as trustees of various funds, *but the moral implications of how those funds were invested.* The principle was that property held by the church should be the servant of human need. The reality is that property and its security often become more important in the minds of those who make decisions than human values.[12]

In response to a resolution proposed by the Council for Christian Social Action, the Synod did establish a Committee on Financial Investments charged with the responsibility to "establish criteria and make recommendations toward substantial use of investments of all national Instrumentalities and Conferences to promote maximum social impact based on established General Synod policies." In the spring of 1970, the Committee's report, "Investing Church Funds for Maximum Social Impact," was circulated throughout the United Church of Christ. The story has already been told of the use of Conference financial resources in Massachusetts to fund the Black Ecumenical Commission.

At the local level, another example is found in the ability of Cooperative Metropolitan Ministries[13] to persuade trustees of churches and synagogues to invest $52,000 of church funds at

---

[12] That fact is particularly transparent within the local church. After fire had destroyed its building, the Eliot Church of Newton was rebuilt in 1957 at a cost of $800,000. The sum of $300,000 was realized from insurance and agencies and individuals within the Newton community, leaving the members of the church with the need to raise $500,000. By the end of 1962 that debt was completely amortized. However, no one would even imagine that a similar amount of money could be raised for "human investments" and that is precisely the question that is at the heart of the Black Manifesto.

[13] Cooperative Metropolitan Ministries is a consortium of 39 Protestant and Roman Catholic churches and synagogues in metropolitan Boston working together in the inner city. The story of C.M.M. can be found in: Harold R. Fray, Jr., *Conflict and Change in the Church* (Philadelphia: Pilgrim Press, 1969), pp. 12-20.

6% interest in a church-related project seeking to be responsive to human needs in one of America's large urban areas. Initiated in January 1966 by the vision and concern of a few members of six local churches, with Charles H. Harper as Executive Director, the impact of Cooperative Metropolitan Ministries was formally acknowledged on May 26, 1970, by the Greater Boston Chamber of Commerce, when, at its Sixty-First Annual Meeting, it presented its annual Distinguished Community Service Award to Earl P. Stevenson with the following citation:

> Through the encouragement and aid of Earl P. Stevenson, Chairman of Cooperative Metropolitan Ministries, Boston soon will be able to point to a model housing rehabilitation project within its Inner City. The Parcel 19 Redevelopment Project in the South End has won both community and local government support as an example of how non-profit groups might proceed in improving the housing situation of the Core City. The creation of a vibrant Emergency Tenants Council and its acceptance by the predominantly Puerto Rican neighborhood and by the Boston Redevelopment Authority will insure a minimum of disruption to the area earmarked for rehabilitation.
>
> Mr. Stevenson's dedication to this commendable project and to the overall housing and urban renewal program in Boston qualifies the former President of the Greater Boston Chamber of Commerce as the recipient of this year's Distinguished Community Service Award.

Action by the Ohio Conference of the United Church of Christ also reflects a particularly imaginative and potent form of response by the church in the area of fiscal and social responsibility. By a vote of 223 "for," 84 "against," and 78 "abstaining" the delegates to the conference's annual meeting in 1970 took action against the Gulf Oil Corporation.

Citing that the Gulf Oil Corporation "through oil operations royalties, contributes almost half of the cost involved for Portugal to sustain her war against the African people of Angola, Mozambique and Guinea (Bissau) to keep them in colonial status," thereby providing "the support for the suppression of the African national liberation movements which are fighting to bring freedom and independence to their countries," the UCC Ohio Conference made recommendations to its constituent churches:

> . . . . that members using Gulf Oil products discontinue the use of those products until Gulf Oil discontinues the use of its African operations in ways that cause human suppression and suffering;
> . . . . encourages all delegates attending this 1970 Annual Meeting to turn in any Gulf Oil credit cards, [and] recommends a similar action to be instituted in its member congregations;

. . . . recommends to all United Church of Christ members in this Conference that they *not* sell stock which they may own in Gulf Oil, but that they exercise the voting power of their stock in order to develop humane policies with regard to Gulf Oil's African operations.

Affronted by this action, B. R. Dorsey, president of Gulf Oil Corporation, demanded "an immediate retraction of the resolution by the conference." In a July 27, 1970 letter to the past president of the Ohio Conference the president of Gulf said:

> Our attorneys have been asked to determine what legal actions should be taken to obtain redress for the damages done to Gulf Oil Corporation and to the reputation of its principal officers by the dissemination of the defamatory document.

Under threat of this suit by the Gulf Corporation the directors of the Ohio Conference reviewed the action taken by the delegates to the annual meeting and in a statement adopted December 4, 1970 affirmed its support of the resolution directed against Gulf. It did challenge, however, the "singular culpability" of the Gulf Oil Corporation, finding, through its study, many "factors contributing to the repression of the Angolan people's legitimate desire for self-determination, including other American corporate entities engaged in profit-making ventures in Angola."

During this period of crisis the Council for Christian Social Action of the United Church of Christ offered its staff services to the Ohio Conference and on December 3, 1970, adopted its own resolution "opposing Gulf Oil Corporation's presence in Angola."

On the matter of more equitable age representation, this priority of United Churchmen for Change was formally presented by a Synod delegate requesting that appropriate bylaw changes be drafted to insure that all Instrumentalities, Councils, Committees, Commissions, and Conference delegates to the General Synod of 1973 be equally represented in accord with the following age-groups:

1. Fifteen to thirty years of age;
2. Thirty-one to forty-five years of age;
3. Forty-six and above.

After considerable debate affirmative action by the delegates included the following:

> The General Synod instructs the newly elected Executive Council to prepare bylaw and rule provisions to assure that persons under 30 years of age constitute at least 20% of the representatives to the General Synod of the United Church of Christ and to the governing

boards for the membership of the Instrumentalities, Councils, Committees, and Commissions.

Even before being voted as a legal requirement the impact of this action has had a significant effect upon delegate representation to the Eighth General Synod of 1971. In 1969 there were less than 10 Synod delegates under 30 years of age; in 1971 there were more than 135.

The third concern for the development of resources and programs at the grassroots level of the church was rejected in the motions presented to the Seventh General Synod. Once again, however, an idea that has come of age cannot be denied. Regional hearings held by the Mission Priorities Council of the United Church of Christ in 1970 discovered that local church and leadership development was one of the principal areas of concern within the church; thereby assuring that it would be a primary focal point for the Eighth General Synod. Convened in Grand Rapids, Michigan in June 1971, the delegates to the Synod acted favorably upon the recommendation of the UCC Executive Council:

> That the President of the Church create and organize a task force to inquire into the whole matter of ways by which the national arm of the UCC, in concert with the conferences, can better serve the local churches through the development of leadership, both clergy and lay, and thus assist them in strengthening their life and mission.

The creation of this Presidential Task Force is a clear indication of the concern for leadership training and organizational development within the church; topics which are the foci of chapters 4 and 5 of this book.

If the Seventh General Synod opened new cracks within the United Church of Christ—to the embarrassment, the anger, and the birth of new hope for some—it was the 1970 United Church Assembly convened in Milwaukee, February 1-3, that laid bare the deeper levels of pain and anguish, as church members and leaders struggle to be faithful to Christ in the latter third of the twentieth century. The challenge came in two potent forms.

The first was public welfare. This issue—through the prodding of Father Groppi and others—has long been associated with Wisconsin and Milwaukee in particular. The Christian Education Council, a national association of Christian educators, made welfare central to the United Church Assembly. Convening just prior to the Assembly, their Christian consciences and grief over manifest injustice to the poor, prompted them to issue a public statement in support of welfare mothers. That was followed by a march through the streets of downtown Milwaukee in support of the demands of those on public welfare. Many Assembly delegates joined the demonstration. The hostility that etched the faces of those who lined the sidewalks watching the march in support of the demands of those on public welfare, made it clear that the church was confronting the world in a painful and challenging way.

The second occasion for confrontation came in the business meetings of the Council for Christian Social Action. The adopted agenda came to an abrupt halt when Stephen Larson, a young draft resister working in Milwaukee, presented himself before the Council, asking that this particular church agency receive his draft card as an act of their support of his personal, Christian witness. Mr. Larson, appealing for the support of the Council members, said:

> I am here to ask you to join in an act of moral resistance to the military draft . . . also to the growing militarism which I hope we all see in our country.

Recognizing that members of the Council might have an innate suspicion of him, he confessed:

> I am somewhat suspicious of you. All too many times I have seen good people, young and old, black and white, radical and conservative, cut themselves off both physically and mentally from a person who begins to talk about a controversial subject.

He added:

> I plead with you to listen and to conscientiously act upon the subject of draft resistance, a subject which to many men of my age is the most profound and critical decision of our lives.

After enumerating his many objections to United States policy in Southeast Asia, Mr. Larson asked:

> Did our knowledge, demonstrations, debates, or statements really change the basic murderous, controlling policy of our government? Is Vietnamization really a change in the war policy? I say, it is not.

His analysis, he said, led him to an inevitable conclusion:

> The reaction to immoral policy must be moral. Facing the draft demands ultimately, sooner or later, a life-decision. When you have no control over government policy, you are left with morally controlling your own life. I ask you to join with me in this act of non-cooperation and to actively support the moral resistance from welfare to warfare to the military draft.

Reminiscent of Martin Luther before the Diet of Worms, Mr. Larson ended his dramatic appeal in a poignant manner:

> Today, I unburden myself of this draft card, to me a symbol of this country's militarism, in the presence of a church body which has taken stands on the pressing issues of our times.

After much anguished, soul-searching discussion, the members of the Council, in a split-vote, agreed to receive Steve Larson's draft card and transmit it to the Department of Justice in Washington, D.C.—perhaps providing the first occasion in which an agency of a denomination has acted out its commitment to peace in this particular way. That evening a spontaneous service of worship took place in the ballroom of the Sheraton-Schroeder Hotel, as delegates to the Assembly and friends of Steve Larson came together to celebrate the witness of a young man and the action of a church instrumentality. The vitality of that experience, rooted in the crisis of a particular event, was a significant departure from the routine worship services experienced by most Sunday after Sunday.

Understandably not all delegates to the Assembly were equally enthusiastic about the action of the Christian Education Council in support of those on public welfare and the decision by the Council for Christian Social Action to receive a draft card. The cup of joy for some produced dregs of bitterness for others. The anguish of some found expression in a letter sent to all UCC churches in Wisconsin by the conference president, Ralph P. Ley.

> The Mid-Winter Assembly of the United Church of Christ concluded its sessions yesterday afternoon and already there have been repercussions because of some newspaper publicity of activities that took place. Therefore, I'm glad for the opportunity to write you this personal note, as I usually do after each annual meeting of the Conference and after the meeting of General Synod.
>
> You must remember that the Mid-Winter Assembly is not a legislative delegated body, representing our churches or our Conference. It is the meeting of denominational boards and agencies gathered in one location, meeting separately for their own business but coming together at stated times for an all-agency denominational presentation. It is held annually as a planning session and this year it was held in Milwaukee with about four hundred people in attendance.
>
> This year's Assembly featured the installation of Dr. Robert Moss as the president of our denomination. The service of installation combined both traditional and contemporary features and most of those in attendance felt it was a very meaningful service. Twenty-three hundred people were present, most of them from our Wisconsin Conference. I was both pleased and proud of our Conference

and I want to personally thank all those who either participated or made a special effort to be present. We sponsored a hospitality corner for those who attended the various meetings and many visitors expressed appreciation for it. Almost thirty of our churches were hosts to deputation teams from these national boards and agencies and these people returned with glowing reports about how well they were received by these churches! We are grateful to these churches too. Many of our people attended discussions, hearings and other programs during the past few days and this demonstrated the alert interest of our membership, both lay and clergy, in the issues facing our church today.

However, there was some unfavorable response to the statements and activities of a few small groups who attended the Assembly. For example, the Christian Education Council, a voluntary association of Christian Educators from all over the country, felt compelled to make a statement about the welfare situation in Milwaukee. In the first place, this outside group knew very little of what we have been doing to face this issue before they came. Then, they released a newspaper statement which said they felt that thievery and vandalism by welfare mothers at two Milwaukee stores was "justified." We strenuously objected to this and called the two major newspapers in Milwaukee indicating that we disagreed with this statement that the end justifies the means. We said also, that stop-gap measures were not the final solution for welfare recipients. They do not strike at the basic causes of the welfare problem; and this latter is one of our concerns as a Conference. We have long been interested in this urgent social problem. We resented the implications and attitudes exhibited by this outside group even though only twenty or thirty people were involved, and they were speaking simply for themselves.

Again, there was the matter of the young man turning in his draft card. Most of us do not agree with this particular procedure and many of us would regard it as unpatriotic. However our Conference continues to agonize with our young people in the decisions they must make about an unpopular war and the draft. Only fourteen people of the Council of Christian Social Action voted to receive the draft card and they made it plain they represented only themselves. Many of our members resent this action, yet a significant number of our youth felt it was evidence that the U.C.C. was truly relevant. Whatever your personal attitude may be, I urge you to ponder the issues this activity brings into focus.

Some of our people have expressed concern about statements made by Robert V. Moss, the newly installed President of the United Church of Christ. Many of us do not agree with some of the statements he has made but he must have the freedom and privilege of making them if he is to serve our church adequately. One of his own sons has been seriously wounded in Vietnam and is being returned one hundred percent disabled. Further, I wish I had the time to tell you about the enormous pressures being placed on him by various groups within our denomination. We must be patient and understanding for he is basically a brilliant and compassionate man and he wants to steer a stable, solid and firm course in the midst of this pressure. His leadership will be effective, but we must not be too critical in these days of unusual, and often unreasonable, pressures church leaders face.

There were other statements and activities which made some of us very unhappy; but, we must not be too disturbed by them. After all, we have a long history of living and serving together through controversy and crisis. Our Christian fellowship is strong enough to contain diverse opinions and opposing views as it has been from the time of Christ Himself. Even though we may disagree with the activities and statements of some, we must understand that they are endeavoring to fulfill the will of God as they see it. So as Paul said in his day, we must be "steadfast" and "keep the faith" and be united in the one Body of Christ. In these days, we can not afford anything less.

The Wisconsin Conference is spiritually strong and healthy enough to take these differing opinions and actions by some groups without being disrupted or fragmented. We must permit others to express their convictions without rancor or divisiveness, even though these convictions may be diametrically opposed to our own. This is the strength, as well as the heritage of our denomination. I know of several churches within our Conference which were stations of the underground railroad in Civil War days. Not everyone agreed with their activity and many thought them to be unpatriotic. Every age has similar examples of this kind of activism.

I feel that the Wisconsin Conference is a leader in the concern for justice and peace. This year our budget calls for over $150,000 for urban problems alone. We want to maintain this ministry in the name of Christ no matter how intemperate and difficult various factions within our denomination may seem to be. Let us respond to Christ's compassionate call to service so that nothing will deter us from this common cause.

With sincere Christian greetings,

Ralph P. Ley, President
Wisconsin Conference

The pain and joy of ministry touches the church at every level of its life. Can we learn from it? Can we prepare for it? Can we better equip men and women for ministry in the decades of the 70's and 80's?

Chapter 3
MAKING MINISTRY POSSIBLE

If you have raced with men on foot,
and they have wearied you,
how will you compete with horses?
And if in a safe land you fall down,
how will you do in the jungle of the Jordan?
  Jeremiah 12:5

From the preceding pages it is clear that ministry today is often caught in the maelstrom of an *ecclesiastical jungle.* Expectations of both clergy and laity are in transition, frequently in conflict, for "the times, they are changing." There is polarization; the exposure of raw nerve ends and the stretching of human capacities to the breaking point, and beyond. On all sides our "clay feet" are showing. We know "we have this treasure in earthen vessels (2 Cor. 4:7)," but there is increasing evidence that the traditional ecclesiastical pots of the past are not adequate for the Christian ministry of the day. Those who received their seminary degrees in prior years must now be taught new skills—and that maxim applies to all professional leaders at every level of vocational involvement. The problems confronting the church today are systemic and inclusive. Those who are now in seminaries must be given new and better resources in order to be equipped for the tasks that will fall to them. And those who sit in positions of power and influence within the church bureaucracy and those who sit in the pews must develop a new seriousness about the kinds of support structures required to make the ministry possible and viable for those exposed to the risks and hazards of serving in the local parish.

THE HUMAN POTENTIAL MOVEMENT

Out of this recognized need there is developing new resources for both clergy and laity. One avenue is the cultivation of new skills and understanding through the Human Potential Movement, which is gaining increasing popularity and notoriety, and providing new experiences in human growth and development for people in all walks of life. Dozens of "human growth centers" are now established across the country, universities have

79

added human relations centers, and skilled leadership in this area is increasingly being employed by churches and institutions of public education.

In the summer of 1971, under the auspices of the Board for Homeland Ministries of the United Church of Christ, twenty experienced husband and wife teams were selected to receive additional training in the theory and methods of the human potential movement. The focus of the training was not psychological —though that played an important part—but a theological understanding of the nature of man and his capacities to love and be loved, based on a research design to gather data on the uses of such training within the church by husband and wife teams. The intent was to increase the number of skilled people in the church who could utilize the insights of the human potential movement for Christian ministry.

It is generally acknowledged that the movement traces its roots to Kurt Lewin, a psychologist of the Massachusetts Institute of Technology, and the initiation of the first T-group (T meaning training) at Bethel, Maine, in 1947. With the proliferation of growth and training centers that have followed, the summer programs that continue to meet at Bethel under the direction of the National Training Laboratories (NTL) remain among the best known and most respected in the country. Inevitably the movement has expanded into many forms depending upon the orientation and skills of the leadership and the goals of the participants. The most common classifications include T-groups, sensitivity groups, encounter groups, sensory awareness groups, gestalt groups, and organizational development groups. The latter is more institutionally oriented than the personal growth and development groups. The next chapter will examine organizational changes and their potential effect upon the church.

Variations within the human potential movement, accompanied by burgeoning popularity,[1] have produced experimentation

---

[1] The La Jolla center in San Diego issued invitations to persons throughout Southern California to participate in groups with facilitators in training. To the amazement of all, 600 people showed up for the first weekend and 800 for the second. In the first three years of the program, approximately 8,000 people have been involved in these weekend groups. One knowledgeable leader estimates that in 1970, 750,000 individuals participated in some form of intensive group experience. These statistics are reported by Carl Rogers, *Carl Rogers on Encounter Groups* (New York: Harper & Row, 1970), pp. 149, 154-55.

and behavior that have stimulated the fears of many and resulted in distorted reporting in the press. Stories in the news media have frequently left the reader, who does not have other sources of information, with the impression that many groups engage in nakedness and sexual permissiveness. While it is true that such activities have occurred, groups that stress freedom of expression through "nude marathons" constitute less than one tenth of one percent of group experiences within the human potential movement.[2]

An even greater anxiety is the fear that extensive emotional and psychological damage will be done to group participants by unskilled and inadequately trained leaders.[3] While the goal of fully qualified leadership should always be a high priority, present research indicates that the fear of psychic damage to individuals is exaggerated.

The La Jolla center, which brought together 8,000 persons on a random basis in a three-year period, to participate under a variety of facilitators in training, reports "no psychological breakdown of any kind during the weekends."[4]

The report adds:

> There have been, much later, two instances of a psychic break in participants in the program. It is a question whether this is more than would normally occur in any equal number of the population over the same period of time.[5]

When Carl Rogers made a systematic follow-up with 481 persons who had participated in group experiences he had led, his inquiry yielded the following results:

> Two felt that the experience had been mostly damaging and had changed their behavior in ways they did not like. A moderate number felt that the experience had been rather neutral or had made no perceptible change in their behavior. Another moderate number felt that it had changed their behavior, but that this change had largely disappeared. The overwhelming majority felt that it had been constructive in its results, or had been a deeply meaningful positive ex-

---

[2] Ibid., p. 6.

[3] The more conscientious within the movement are concerned for regulations and standards. The Third New England Conclave for Applied Behavioral Scientists meeting in Durham, New Hampshire, January 24, 1970, brought together over 300 leaders, representing many facets of the movement. Much attention was given to the subject of standards, but at the moment the newness of the movement and its many variations defy standardization and regulations.

[4] Rogers, op. cit., p. 155.

[5] Ibid.

perience which made a continuing positive difference in their behavior.[6]

Extensive research on intensive group experiences, covering a wide range of techniques and leadership, has been done by Jack R. Gibb. From his work he draws the following conclusions:

> The evidence is strong that intensive group-training experiences have therapeutic effects. . . .
> Changes do occur in sensitivity, feeling management, directionality of motivation, attitudes toward the self, attitudes toward others, and interdependence. . . .
> The evidence is clear that the reputed dangers of sensitivity training are greatly exaggerated. . . .
> Groups grow under a variety of conditions, with or without leaders, and when this growth occurs, behavior change can happen. . . .
> Evidence indicates that the following optimal conditions for learning occur with group growth: feedback, behavior visibility, member-member interaction, feeling expression, and perceptual diversity. . . .
> The behavior of the trainer can make a difference. His influence is determined, in part, by the amount of self-disclosure, help-orientation, participation in person-oriented feedback, and process interventions. . . .
> Significant findings that human-relations training, under some conditions, produces changes that seem to increase with time, seems to mean that initial periods of training must be long enough for persons to "learn to learn" from feedback or to reach a critical point at which internal organismic processes occur in the individual, which sustain change. . . .
> Research evidence indicates no basis for making any restrictions as to group membership.[7]

These conclusions are important to bear in mind as encounter groups increasingly find their appropriate place in the ministry of the church. Ungrounded fears of something new and different threaten to cut off a very important resource and method of learning and growth for both clergy and laity.

Because the fears of emotional, personality damage have been so pervasive (perhaps reflecting nothing more than a defense mechanism against the unknown) it is important to extend this review to Rogers' own observations that "not only the layman, but often the psychologist or psychiatrist not involved in groups,

---

[6] Ibid., p. 126.

[7] Jack R. Gibb, "The Effects of Human Relations Training," in Allen E. Bergin and Sol L. Garfield, editors, *Handbook of Psychotherapy and Behavior Change* (New York: John Wiley & Sons, 1971), pp. 855-57. Used by permission of John Wiley & Sons, Inc.

can come up with many 'horror stories' about the terribly disturbing psychological effects of groups." [8]

Gibb reports a study "made to uncover harmful effects of group training upon approximately 1,200 YMCA directors who had intensive experiences in sensitivity training," [9] with the following results:

> First, they found that executives who had not had such training reported widespread rumors of traumatic effects of such training upon YMCA directors they had heard about. The investigators were able to find only four out of 1,200 cases that were supposed to be negative. Intensive interviewing revealed that three of these four cases turned out to be positive. Only one case still evaluated his experience as a "negative" one, and he continues to do an effective job in his position as a YMCA director. [10]

THE HUMAN POTENTIAL MOVEMENT IN THE CHURCH

In relationship to the church, one study of encounter groups as a tool of growth and ministry has been done by Gerald and Elisabeth Jud and another by Howard J. Clinebell. [11] The importance of the Jud study, based on a series of three-day "shalom retreats" held at Kirkridge, a retreat and study center in Bangor, Pennsylvania, lies in several directions. It provides a basis for examining the human potential movement when combined with a Christian value system. It provides new insights into the transmission of the Christian gospel, in which the proclamation of the biblical faith is experienced in a new way. Faith comes alive, and with it comes a whole new concept of worship and celebration. Most important of all there is clear evidence of changed behavior, which bears out the conclusions of the studies made by Gibb, and has incalculable importance in pointing the way toward teaching clergy and laity new skills and new ability to cope with the complex problems of Christian ministry today. Encounter groups are not a cure-all for the problems facing the church—they will not answer all the needs of the professional minister—but they are a resource which the church will neglect only to its own detriment. My personal experience, both

---

[8] Rogers, op. cit., p. 120.

[9] Gibb, op. cit., p. 856.

[10] Ibid.

[11] Gerald and Elisabeth Jud, *Training in the Art of Loving* (Philadelphia: Pilgrim Press, 1972); and Howard J. Clinebell, Jr., *The People Dynamic* (New York: Harper & Row, 1971).

as a participant in encounter groups and as a leader, bears this out.

Because this is a new area of exploration for many in the church, perhaps a word about my own experience in encounter groups would illuminate some of its potential and meaning.

The nature of my Christian ministry over a period of almost two decades has embroiled me in continuous conflict. Believing that the church exists for the world—and not for its own institutional self-preservation—I have sought to provide a style of leadership requiring interaction between the ethical imperatives of the Christian gospel and the pressing human needs of our society. The results have been controversy and conflict. At stake for me personally has been the preservation of my own job as minister of a local church and an inner capacity to deal with the anger and hostility that my ministry has generated. With the support of many parishioners, I have been successful in the former; but less so with the latter.

Each of us is conditioned to handle unpleasant events and emotions that are directed against us. For me it was not a conscious choice but an innate response. I built a wall. It was not visible to the eye, but it was perceived by those who knew me best. My severest critics complained that it did no good to talk with me, for I seemed determined to pursue my chosen course of action. I rationalized that I was not persuaded by their arguments, but I suspect that often they were more rebuffed by the barrier I had created to protect myself emotionally than by my actions. In hindsight, I confess that I refused to allow some to "get to me" for I did not know how to handle their anger and hostility that frequently accompanied their reasoning. My closest friends asked, "Do they issue suits of armor when you graduate from seminary?" I laughed, but it was no laughing matter. Neither my critics nor my friends penetrated my wall, and in the eyes of many of my peers I enjoyed a "successful ministry." Issues between the church and the world were being confronted through my leadership, things were being accomplished, but something else was going on—gradually, steadily—of which I was unaware.

The barrier that I had created to protect myself was so successful that it *walled out my wife.* Her awareness of the barricade between us came at a time when our children were making less demands upon her as they developed and became more independent. That was accompanied by a growing sense of emotional isolation from her minister husband. Desperately she tried to break through, but the walls were too thick. I heard her words and responded with logical arguments, *but I did not feel her pain,* for I had learned to filter out the emotions I could not handle. That was the condition, and the personal agenda I brought to an encounter group.

The participants were ministers and their wives, who also brought their own pain and anger and fear out of the jungle of Christian ministry. Together—if enough trust and openness could develop—we would share our experiences in the church. For me, the initial encounter was a "head trip." That was the arena of human interaction to which I had confined myself in order to survive in the vocation of clergyman. I could talk about feelings, but there was no effect. It was not a lack of desire on my part to express feelings and be fully human. I was a prisoner inside the protective walls I had created. Others could not break in, *but I could not break out.*

My status was obvious to the group members. No doubt my body language betrayed me,[12] as well as my words disassociated from feelings. But the moment of truth and awareness had not yet come to me. One member of the group suggested that the men link arms and form a wall around me, symbolizing my condition. I was familiar with such techniques, and readily assented. I looked at one, and then another of my fellow ministers. Suddenly it was no longer a game. With a burst of energy and strength that came from the core of my being, I broke through the human wall around me and lay on the floor crying hysterically. The dam had been broken. When the flood of tears subsided, I rolled over on my back to discover that I was surrounded by smiling men and women who reached out and placed their hands upon me. (I now know why the church honors the practice of "the laying on of hands." Unfortunately, in the church today, the practice is a ritual devoid of meaning.) With their hands upon me, I again felt connected to the human community in a loving, accepting way, *and for the first time in an indeterminate number of years, I was neither ashamed nor afraid of my deeper feelings.* More was yet to come; much more.

---

[12] Insight on how we communicate nonverbally, through the body, can be found in Julius Fast, *Body Language* (New York: M. Evans, 1970).

A fissure in my protective shell was now letting in some light, but it was several hours later, with this same group, before the wall was fully breached. The experience illustrates another facet of what happens in encounter groups that facilitates growth and development: we learn and share vicariously. One man talked about the goals and aspirations of his ministry. By chance (or would it be better to say by the grace and design of God?) I was sitting in a position where I could look at him as he talked, and could also see his wife seated behind him. As he talked about his tasks of Christian ministry, his involvements, his conflicts, my attention was increasingly drawn to the face of his wife. As he talked about their family life, what I saw registered on her face did not match his words. When he concluded, I asked her if she would be willing to share with all of us what she thought about her husband's statements, particularly his observations about their life together. I was unaware of what I was subconsciously asking of her.

With understandable hesitation, she began to speak about her own feelings in relationship to her minister husband. Suffice it to say, he was shocked, but the impact of her words upon me were overpowering. *She was speaking, but it was my own wife that I was listening to for the first time.* The pain was excruciating. I began to hear what my wife had been trying to tell me for a very long time. My shell had produced emotional isolation for her. She had tried repeatedly to communicate her sense of separateness. She expressed feelings of inadequacy which I dismissed knowing what a very competent person she is. I, too, stood under the edict of Isaiah:

> Hear and hear, but do not understand;
> see and see, but do not perceive.
>   Isaiah 6:9

Now I heard.

Since that moment, we have been building our marriage anew. Like many couples after 20 years of marriage we had three choices: (1) settle into the well-grooved rut we had established—(thank God my wife was too strong to tolerate that); (2) go our separate ways—(we had too much that was positive and meaningful in our marriage to accept that); or (3) begin a new marriage together—(that has become the new possibility for us). It has not all been uphill, but there has been a new reality in our lives, as we seek to share the full range of our personhood with one another. We understand George Bach and his associates who specialize in training couples to fight fairly. Bach and Wyden write:

> We believe . . . that there can be no mature intimate relationship without aggressive leveling; that is, "having it out," speaking up, asking the partner "what's eating" him and negotiating for realistic settlements of differences. This does cause stress, but . . . the pain of conflict is the price of true and enduring love.[13]

It was this emotional interrelatedness that my protective shell had made impossible. My wife confesses the fault was not all mine. Her own heritage compounded our problem. She grew up in a home where one communicated by words but rarely expressed feelings. Her words had not penetrated my wall and her feelings had remained repressed. The husband/wife relationship is critical for the professional clergyman. The study done for the United Church of Christ on ex-pastors indicates that the wife is the single most important factor in determining the viability of her husband's ministry.[14]

The experiences described above and the new dynamics in my own marriage have been central to my developing ministry. I doubt very much if I would have risked the vulnerability of stepping down from the pulpit on Sunday, May 3, 1970, and sitting on the chancel steps (see page 27), if I had not developed some new degree of openness. When appropriate I express my anger in church meetings, and I find that I sleep better at night. When in need, I ask for help, and have discovered many ready to offer support. Over the years I have missed much in human relationships with my parishioners by seeking to project a false adequacy. I now realize that I am more capable of Christian ministry when I am more human and therefore more accessible to others.

The human potential movement, and encounter groups in particular, provide the church with an effective tool in developing and strengthening the bonds between husbands and wives.

It is equally significant as a means of communicating the

---

[13] George R. Bach and Peter Wyden, *The Intimate Enemy* (New York: William Morrow & Co., 1969), p. 13.

[14] Gerald J. Jud, Edgar W. Mills, Jr., Genevieve Walters Burch, *Ex-Pastors: Why Men Leave the Parish Ministry* (Philadelphia: Pilgrim Press, 1970), p. 64.

reality of the Christian gospel. The biblical message is experienced. For my wife and me, the meaning of crucifixion and resurrection has a new dimension and depth. For years, I have read the stories about Jesus casting out demons and passed over them. Now I have seen the demons of fear, anger, and pain exorcized, giving room for self-acceptance, love, and inner peace.

There are risks because genuine encounter with persons requires vulnerability. But all growth demands risking. There is a need for openness that necessitates trust . . . but trust and love are something the Christian church claims to know something about. The Christian community must be a place where the promises of the gospel are experienced; otherwise we give stones to those who ask for bread. The human potential movement provides a new resource for the church. The evidence of human need is all about us. The words of one seminary student are not atypical:

> *disquiet. the unspeakable pain of distance—no breath, no movement. I am defined—apart.*

> *yes. destroy the walls and amid the mess and rubble remaining, accept the rainbow that was there all the time—that passed through the walls.*

> *why are they so high?*
> *are they my walls?*
> *am I their creator—the master of their demon builders?*

> *no. separation is my state—my dung-heap of anxiety and crushed life. it is my death. surrounded yet alone. loved yet unable to love. ice—pain—they are mine.*

> *help me break the embittered barriers that define my life. I am dying without you.*

> *sweep over those walls and awaken me like ocean winds giving life to grasses—rushes/waves—movement.*

> *make the harmony that I know yet cannot realize live within me. finish off the circle—complete it. it can be made again—made to expand, flourish, expand, flourish, expand, breathe.*

> *no. not alone—but through the otherside it is possible. here is just helpless suffering—weakness. here I am.*

> *receive this mess I call myself and pull it back through the center —into place—unity.*

> *make it one.*

> *make it clear—confusing, fast, chaotic, whirling, upending, furious —at peace.*

clear, ravished quiet—after my storm, if I last that long.

   restore me.

   —BCJ [15]

The need penetrates the whole of our society. It is rooted in a hunger for community and intimacy. In the appraisal of Carl Rogers, the rapid growth of encounter groups represents a "demand by people clearly seeking something." [16] He describes their search in the following way:

> I believe it is a hunger for something the person does not find in his work environment, in his church, certainly not in his school or college, and sadly enough, not even in modern family life. It is a hunger for relationships which are close and real; in which feelings and emotions can be spontaneously expressed without first being carefully censored or bottled up; where deep experiences—disappointments and joys—can be shared; where new ways of behaving can be risked and tried out; where, in a word, he approaches the state where all is known and all accepted, and thus further growth becomes possible.[17]

How sharply these human needs illuminate the vocation of the church, and demonstrate where we have failed. As the institutional church opens itself to this resource for learning and growing, it will make a significant step in providing the kind of support structures for both clergy and laity that makes the Christian ministry a daring, exciting possibility in the coming decade of change and turmoil.

FREMONT, NEBRASKA: TESTING GROUND OF AN INSTITUTIONAL SUPPORT STRUCTURE

Multiple resources are required within the church to stimulate and support effective, creative Christian ministries. Personal support structures are mandatory. That requires an environment in which there are trust and freedom to express personal need,[18] and a community capable of responding. Institutional support structures are equally critical. We need to know how and where to ask for and receive help in time of need.

---

[15] A confession and petition expressed at a service of worship at the Eliot Church of Newton by Bruce C. Johnson, October 10, 1970.

[16] Rogers, op. cit., p. 10.

[17] Ibid., pp. 10-11.

[18] For many clergymen this means a new self-image, in which they are free to ask the members of their congregations for help, as well as give it.

In the fall of 1967 when I was publically involved with young men who, as an act of conscience, were resisting military induction by turning in or destroying their draft cards, I remembered a strongly worded statement on civil disobedience passed by the annual meeting of the Massachusetts Conference of the United Church of Christ in 1964. As one means of protecting my own exposed flank, I asked Albert J. Penner, then minister and president of the conference, to take that statement and issue it to the press with a personal note related to the stance of young men refusing to fight in the Vietnam War. He readily complied and I felt personally supported. My pastoral role to young men of conscience was placed in a context that helped me interpret my actions to members of the congregation I served.

There is power that can be exercised by church bureaucrats in a significant and supportive way. In the fall of 1969, the International Relations Committee of the United Church of Christ wished to encourage and support participation in the anti-war rally in the nation's capital. Robert V. Moss, Jr., president of the United Church of Christ, was petitioned to lend the support of his office to this effort. In response, Dr. Moss informed the Executive Council of his intentions, then issued a personal invitation to the ministers and presidents of the 40 conferences to join him at the anti-war rally in Washington, D.C. In addition, Dr. Moss presided at the service of worship at the National Cathedral that was held in conjunction with the massive demonstrations. This open, supportive role by the president of the church provided substantial help to those rallying support for the Washington demonstrations in local churches. Too frequently those involved in the struggles against racism and war have felt isolated and deserted by the church's judicatory leaders, who seemed, rightly or wrongly, to be more concerned with institutional preservation and the uninterrupted flow of financial support, than in supporting those who are seeking to act out their moral, ethical convictions on issues that generate conflict and alienation. Church leaders will not always agree on the means employed to confront specific issues, but if there is any meaning to Christian community, it is imperative that we learn how to support one another at every level of the church's operation. Without this support there is a loss of morale, alienation, and for some, rejection of the vocation of Christian ministry.

The story of the First Congregational Church, United Church

of Christ, of Fremont, Nebraska, provides an excellent case study of an effective institutional support structure. It is the saga of a minister under attack by a veterans' organization, and the responses of persons within the community, members of the church he serves and the Nebraska Conference.

In February 1970 Edwin Mehlhaff, pastor of the First Congregational Church, United Church of Christ, Fremont, Nebraska, was invited to speak to 150 students of three history classes in the local high school on the subject of rapid social change. Since coming to Fremont in 1968, Mr. Mehlhaff had spoken before various high school groups on issues related to history, sociology and family living. But the February experience was destined to be different, with consequences that would reverberate throughout the rural Nebraska community. Neighbor would be pitted against neighbor in the kind of public controversy that has wracked many communities in recent years.

In the question period that followed his presentation, Mr. Mehlhaff was asked what he thought about Vietnam. Realizing the potential implications of the question, the minister asked the teaching staff whether he should digress into such a subject. One teacher replied, "Ours is a free class room and our kids are free to ask whatever they want." With that assurance, Mr. Mehlhaff indicated that a recent poll showed 40% of the American people opposing the war in Southeast Asia, and he shared their opinion. A second question followed, "Would you tell young men to avoid the draft?" Without hesitation, the Fremont minister replied that he would not counsel anyone to undertake a specific course of action; rather he would explore with a person the options open to him and the potential consequences of his decision. Then came the final query, "Would you go if you were drafted?" With appropriate candor, Mr. Mehlhaff said, "That's asking a 40-year-old man to answer a question faced by 18-year-olds. But if at 18 I thought the way I think now, I would not go."

That series of interchanges occurred in February 1970. In September 1970 an article appeared in a local newspaper indicating that Mr. Mehlhaff had responded affirmatively to a request by the National Council of Churches to serve as a pastoral resource person to families whose sons had refused induction into the armed forces and fled to Canada.

The stage was set. In early December 1970 the Henry Teigeler, Jr. Post No. 20 of the American Legion was reported to have sent a letter to the Board of Education of the Fremont School District raising some serious questions about the Rev. Mr. Mehlhaff's ministry. A newspaper story printed in the *Fremont Guide and Tribune* on December 4, 1970, reported that: (1) "recent newspaper stories indicate that Rev. Mehlhaff, Minister of U.C.C. Church of Fremont, is an official advisor to draft avoiding 'emigrants' and their families." (2) That the Legion strongly protests "permitting one who is admittedly advising with those who flaunt our country's laws by evading the draft, being called in to advise and counsel with our youth." (3) That Mr. Mehlhaff "has, at the invitation of representatives of our high school, been addressing and counseling with students in our high school." (4) That the Legion's Commander doesn't "think someone like this should be talking to our kids."

Once again a bomb had burst in middle America and it threatened to splinter a community. Mr. Mehlhaff did not receive a copy of the letter and was first informed of it by a reporter of the *Tribune* who read it to him over the telephone. With shocked anger, the United Church minister blurted out, "They're a sick bunch." With the wisdom of hindsight, it was a response he regrets, for in the subsequent controversy that developed, his characterization of the Legion Post became as much an issue for some, as the Legion's accusations against his alleged activities.

The newspaper printed the Legion letter, referring to its allegations against Mr. Mehlhaff as if they were facts. Community and church responses were swift. On Monday, December 7, Mr. Mehlhaff demanded a public retraction by the American Legion Post, charging that Myron Carlson, Commander, had made

> statements regarding my person which will have to be answered on the basis of fact and not his rumor factory. Furthermore, the Legion has libeled itself by allowing the publication of Carlson's statement which is a personal attack attempting to discredit my citizenship in this community, my patriotism to my country, and jeopardizes my effectiveness as a Christian teacher and counselor.[19]

He went on to say:

> Unless the American Legion makes a public retraction of its unfounded charges, my legal counsel advises me that I have more than ample cause to file suit for libel.[20]

---

[19] *Omaha World Herald*, December 8, 1970.
[20] Ibid.

Calling Carlson's letter an "irresponsible emotional outburst," [21] Mehlhaff added the following statement of his counseling practices and principles:

> I have not counseled even one young man at Fremont High or at the church, nor in my own home, to avoid the draft. My counseling principles do not manipulate people into puppetry.[22]

At a later date, Mr. Mehlhaff also demanded a public retraction by the *Fremont Tribune* for printing the unsubstantiated Legion charges as if they were factual. The newspaper quickly responded to the request.

At the scheduled meeting of the Fremont School Board on Monday evening, December 7, a crowd of 150 persons were in attendance and expressed overwhelming support of the Fremont UCC minister. At the same meeting a support statement for Mr. Mehlhaff was read, signed by 16 Fremont ministers. But it was to the members of his own congregation and the Nebraska UCC Conference that Mr. Mehlhaff looked for his primary support. He did not look in vain.

At their own initiative, the council of the church served by Mehlhaff met on December 10, 1970, and took the following action:

1. Expressed their strong support of their minister.

2. Hired legal counsel in his behalf.

3. Appointed a six-member committee to deal with the personal issues for the minister and his family that were bound to arise in relationship to the controversy that had been generated within the community.

4. Bought space in the local newspaper in order to make the following support statement:

   The Council of the First Congregational Church, United Church of Christ of Fremont met in special session on Thursday evening, December 10, 1970. We voted unanimous backing of our minister, the Rev. Mr. Edwin Mehlhaff, and expressed sincere belief in his ability to counsel anyone in our church or community seeking his help.

   We support the National Council of Churches in its appointment of the Rev. Mr. Edwin Mehlhaff as contact and counselor for concerned families in this area, and we admire his courage in accepting this difficult responsibility.[23]

---

21 *Fremont Tribune*, December 7, 1970.
22 Ibid.
23 *Fremont Tribune*, December 14, 1970.

The UCC Nebraska Conference reacted to the Fremont crisis in an immediate supportive way. Scott S. Libbey, Conference Minister, indicated his personal availability to the minister and members of the Fremont church. John W. Newman, chairman of the conference board of directors, offered the legal service of a Lincoln law office that specializes in cases of libel.

That was the kind of support that enabled the ministry of the Fremont UCC Church to continue creatively and effectively. For the minister and his family, the weeks following were filled with anguish and pain, *even with the strong, solid support they experienced.* They could not continue to live in the community and escape the coolness, the bitterness and the hostility of some of their fellow citizens. Jesus said:

> Blessed are you when men revile you and persecute you and utter all kinds of evil against you falsely on my account. Rejoice and be glad, for your reward is great in heaven, for so men persecuted the prophets who were before you.
> Matthew 5:11-12

In truth, most of us would prefer to escape that kind of blessedness. Mr. Mehlhaff expressed a portion of his own particular anguish in a statement to the Church Council, "I am truly sorry that there are those of you who are suffering in this happening who would rather not." But in the Christian community we must "bear one another's burdens (Gal. 6:2)" if the ministry is to be a lively option.

For the community of Fremont, the issue was whether people in positions of power and influence would be held responsible for their actions and accusations against their fellow citizens, or be allowed to go unchallenged. To avoid the issue was to encourage a community environment of fear and paralysis. For the minister and members of the Fremont Church it meant a serious consideration of filing a libel suit against American Legion Post No. 20, with a willingness to bear the repercussions.

Seeking both redress and reconciliation, two Legion members of the First Congregational Church, United Church of Christ, arranged a meeting, over the objections of Commander Carlson, between members of the church and the legionnaires. Each party agreed to bring legal counsel to the dialogue set for April 19, 1971. But no dialogue took place. At the outset of the arranged meeting, four lawyers, representing the Legion Post, began making accusations against Mr. Mehlhaff, desiring to place him under oath and proceed with a cross-examination. With heavy hearts, the members of the church departed after 10 minutes and filed a libel petition in the District Court of Dodge County the following day.

On the evening of April 26, 120 families of the church met together, renewing their covenant with one another, and pledging their continued support of Mr. Mehlhaff, offered to recruit other church members in order to do what was necessary to set the record straight in the city of Fremont regarding the allegations made against their minister by the Henry Teigeler, Jr., Post No. 20 of the American Legion. The following week the spring meeting of the Nebraska Conference convened in the Fremont United Church of Christ, "reaffirmed the importance of free and open discussion of pertinent issues in all institutions of society," urged pastors to "counsel with persons on all issues, including the draft, presenting alternatives and respecting the counselees' freedom of choice," and pressed upon all congregations the importance of supporting their ministers as the Fremont Church has done. As this book is completed the outcome of the Fremont story remains an open question.[24]

The Christian community is being tested. Faithfulness to the gospel of Christ means controversy and conflict. It is a painful time for clergy and congregations, but a rare opportunity for growth and development where there is a hard, honest assessment of those things which make ministry possible. As the church confronts the world mistakes will be made, harsh feel-

---

[24] While this book was in production, the $200,000 libel suit filed by the Rev. Edwin Mehlhaff against the Henry Teigeler, Jr., Post No. 20 of the American Legion, and a cross petition filed by the Legion were both dismissed on September 15, 1971, in the Dodge County District Court. This was reported in the *Fremont Tribune* on September 15, 1971.

A statement issued by attorneys for plaintiff and defendant said that the Legion protest concerning Mr. Mehlhaff's speaking to classes in the public school was based on the minister's appointment as "counselor to parents of emigrants who had fled the United States to avoid the draft," but "was not intended to imply that Rev. Mehlhaff was advising persons to evade the draft," and "the Legion had no intention to in any way attack Rev. Mehlhaff personally or his church." Furthermore, "the Legion recognized Rev. Mehlhaff's right to counsel with anyone and to speak his convictions on any public question."

Mr. Mehlhaff's statement that "the Legion was a 'sick bunch'" and inference in the church paper that "the Legion was attacking him and his church" were withdrawn.

ings will be expressed and polarizations will occur. The reality of the gospel will be on trial and some churches will be found wanting. The hard predictions of Jesus will be experienced:

> Do not think that I have come to bring peace on earth. . . . For I have come to set a man against his father, and a daughter against her mother, and a daughter-in-law against her mother-in-law; and a man's foes will be those of his own household.
> Matthew 10:34-36

When accusations were made against their minister, the members of the Fremont congregation could choose to run for cover or gather together as a supporting community to assess the facts and take appropriate action. They could have chosen to ask their leader to quietly leave in order to prevent a fractured church and a divided community. Instead they chose to let the truth stand on its own two feet in the public arena. Minister and congregation were caught in the crunch in Fremont, Nebraska. Their response to crisis is indicative of the trials, in one form or another, that must be anticipated by the Christian fellowship which intends to be a supporting and sustaining community of Christian ministry at this moment in the life of the church.

Chapter 4
POWER TO THE PEOPLE

> When Moses' father-in-law saw all that he was doing for the people, he said, "What is this that you are doing for the people? Why do you sit alone, and all the people stand about you from morning till evening?" And Moses said to his father-in-law, "Because the people come to me to inquire of God; when they have a dispute, they come to me and I decide between a man and his neighbor, and I make them know the statutes of God and his decisions." Moses' father-in-law said to him, "What you are doing is not good. You and the people with you will wear themselves out, for the thing is too heavy for you; you are not able to perform it alone."
> Exodus 18:14-18

"Ever since religion was invented the priests have been in charge, and that is the problem." Those words, spoken by an ecclesiastical bureaucrat, are indicative of the awareness of the need for fundamental changes in the church system. The church has given lip service to "the priesthood of all believers" but created an authoritarian, bureaucratic structure that has exercised management and control *under episcopal and congregational forms of church government*. This ecclesiastical system is now being challenged from the local church through the national denominational structures.

Like educational and political institutions, the church is at that moment when the forces for change in leadership style and organizational forms are inevitable and irresistible. This is still a shock to those in power, *but a reality that must be grasped by those in leadership positions*. The imperative for new styles of leadership and organizational forms is rooted in social changes that have rendered authoritarian leadership and bureaucracy obsolete. It is this new phenomenon, and its implications for the church, that occupy the concerns of this chapter.

Writing in their book *The Temporary Society*, Warren G. Bennis and Philip E. Slater point out "that every age develops an organizational form appropriate to its genius, and that the prevailing form, known by sociologists as bureaucracy . . . is out of joint with contemporary realities." [1] The cause is a society

---

[1] Warren G. Bennis and Philip E. Slater, *The Temporary Society* (New York: Harper & Row, 1968), p. 54.

undergoing such basic, rapid changes, that new responses are required for survival. Again Bennis:

> Our social institutions cannot withstand, let alone cope with, the devastating rate of change without fundamental alterations in the way they negotiate their environments and the way they conduct the main operations of their enterprise.[2]

Under conditions of critical institutional fragmentation, the training and re-training of its leaders at all levels is a sine qua non for the church. Failure to respond to this imperative insures obsolescence. The new environment is chronic change that undermines stability and identity, requiring a new leadership ability and competence. Some of the new requirements are already in focus. Bennis includes the following: a training system to

(1) help us to identify with the adaptive process without fear of losing our identity,

(2) increase our tolerance of ambiguity without fear of losing intellectual mastery,

(3) increase our ability to collaborate without fear of losing our individuality,

(4) develop a willingness to participate in social evolution while recognizing implacable forces.[3]

He adds, "In short, we need an educational system that can help us make a virtue out of contingency rather than one which induces hesitancy or its reckless companion, expedience."[4]

Given the nature of the church, steeped in century-old forms and tradition, the question is: can the church respond? From the perspective of ecclesiastical theology it is important to affirm: *God does not need the church.* God does not need forms and traditions which men have created and cherish. And if the church, in its present forms, is a structure of "dry bones" beyond reformation and renewal, then it will sink into a fossilized state appropriate to its condition, while God creates new means of conveying his truth, love and power. The hope is that the awareness for new styles of leadership and new forms of organization is so acute and so pervasive at every level of the ecclesiastical structure, that the normal and natural forces of resist-

---

[2] Reprinted by special permission from Warren G. Bennis, *Organization Development: Its Nature, Origins, and Prospects* (Reading, Mass.: Addison-Wesley Publishing Co., 1969), p. 18.

[3] Bennis and Slater, op. cit., p. 127.

[4] Ibid.

ance to change will give way to research, training and experimentation drawing upon the growing body of knowledge represented by the human potential movement, organizational development skills and the behavioral sciences. Movement in this direction by segments of the church is already visible.

THE MISSION PRIORITIES COUNCIL

The thrust within the United Church of Christ to make use of the resources of the human potential movement has been documented earlier in the book. The potential for organizational change and development that could affect the entire life of the denomination is symbolized by the creation of a Mission Priorities Council. Like many things the church has done in the past, this could be another form of ecclesiastical window-dressing, with representatives of the power structure meeting together *to insure that nothing basically changes.* Within the United Church of Christ there is evidence, already cited, that the old is giving way to the new. This is not to condemn those who have labored long and hard in the past, but a recognition that a new day brings new needs. Out of a recognition of these new needs the Mission Priorities Council was established by action of the General Synod of the United Church of Christ.

The Council is composed of the presidents of the 40 conferences, the instrumentality executives, a minister and lay representative of the six regional areas of the United Church of Christ, the president of the church and an executive director. To ascertain its own mandate, the Council held regional hearings in 1970 and discovered—to no one's surprise—that the overriding expression of need was the cry for help within the local church in equipping both clergy and laity to meet the new demands and requirements of effective leadership. The pain of inadequacy, the inability to cope, were reported in multiple ways. The challenge before the Council is to find ways—drawing upon the total resources of the United Church of Christ—to meet the crisis.

Experience in the church indicates that it is unwise to hold out false hopes for the Mission Priorities Council. Ecclesiastical bureaucracy may be so entrenched and resistant to change that established church structures are no longer viable. The danger is not that the "gates of hell" shall move the church, but that the winds of the Spirit cannot penetrate encrusted tradition and power. But at the moment there are still many willing to work within the system for reformation. I would align myself with that company for there are some indications of response and change. If new structures are created, some of the old institutional problems will emerge in new forms. If new leaders come to power, pretensions of wisdom will be asserted in new language. In and out of the church man cannot escape the burdens of his own limitations. He can only work to prevent *rigor mortis* from paralyzing the institutional structures he creates in the service of God and man.

WHEN BIG DADDY STEPS DOWN—
THE MOVE TO ADHOCRACY

Foremost among the needs within the church system is to train leadership to cope creatively and perform effectively under the pressures of conflict and to meet the demands for new responses commensurate with the organizational, institutional changes that are occurring at an accelerated pace. The fundamental challenge is to move from a leadership style that is authoritarian and arbitrary to one that is open, flexible and vulnerable. Several years ago many people chuckled when they browsed through the photographs in the book, *The White Collar Zoo*. Those "in charge" were appropriately compared to overbearing and fierce members of the animal kingdom. The book was a witness and commentary upon our understanding of leadership roles.

Most leadership models with which we are familiar, in and out of the church, are based on a pyramid structure in which there is a clearly defined chain of command; often with an impersonal, uncaring relationship between those on *top* and those *below*. At the judicatory, denominational levels of the church system, those in positions of power have frequently acted as benevolent despots, jealous of their prerogatives and seemingly unresponsive to the felt needs of ministers who serve in the local parishes. In their research of why men leave the parish ministry, Jud, et al., report that more than one third of the ex-pastors they interviewed expressed low support from their denominational executives.[5] Within local churches there is also a role expectation by both clergy and laity that often takes the form that *Herr*

---

[5] Gerald J. Jud, Edgar W. Mills, Jr., Genevieve Walters Burch, *Ex-Pastors: Why Men Leave the Parish Ministry* (Philadelphia: Pilgrim Press, 1970), p. 84.

Pastor is in charge. The trauma for many ministers today is that this form of leadership is no longer viable, because it is associated with a bureaucratic, organizational model that is out of date with the needs of the time. Bennis points out that bureaucracy, with its hierarchial leadership model, was indeed appropriate to "the Victorian era," but is archaic in today's world.[6] And no layer of the church system is unaffected, meaning that the problems facing the church are not partial—allowing bandaid solutions—but systemic, requiring major surgery.

What are the guidelines for a new leadership style, as "big daddy" is forced to step down? Slater and Bennis list five:

1. Full and free communication, regardless of rank and power.

2. A reliance on *consensus,* rather than the more customary forms of coercion or compromise to manage conflict.

3. The idea that *influence* is based on technical competence and knowledge rather than on the vagaries of personal whims or prerogatives of power.

4. An atmosphere that permits and even encourages emotional expression as well as task-oriented acts.

5. A basically human bias, one that accepts the inevitability of conflict between the organization and the individual, but that is willing to cope with and mediate this conflict on rational grounds.[7]

The task is not easy for it is rooted in the need to alter what Bennis describes as "the culture" of the church in which "a system of beliefs and values" about acceptable forms of interaction and relating give way to a new leadership style.[8] It requires new role images for both clergy and laity. It holds new possibilities of vocational identity and freedom for the professional clergy who find themselves exhausted and distraught by the "role overload" described by Katz and Kahn in their book, *The Social Psychology of Organization,* and succinctly reported in an article by James D. Anderson, Director of Parish Development for the Episcopal Diocese of Washington, D.C.[9] The process of change in leadership role and style in the church will be difficult and painful. The important thing is to recognize the need, and begin to respond.

The requirement is an educational system that will develop

[6] Bennis, op. cit., p. 19.

[7] Bennis and Slater, op. cit., p. 4.

[8] Bennis, op. cit., p. v.

[9] James D. Anderson, "Pastoral Support of Clergy-Role Development Within Local Congregations," *Pastoral Psychology,* March 1971, pp. 9-14.

interpersonal competencies, enabling church leaders to be at home in the new world that is rapidly taking shape around them. The coping person must embrace the following capacities:

1. Learning how to develop intense and deep human relationships quickly—and learn how to "let go." In other words, learning how to get love, to love, and to lose love;

2. Learning how to enter groups and leave them;

3. Learning what roles are satisfying and how to attain them;

4. Learning how to widen the repertory of feelings and roles available;

5. Learning how to cope more readily with ambiguity;

6. Learning how to develop a strategic comprehensibility of a new "culture" or system and what distinguishes it from other cultures; and finally,

7. Learning how to develop a sense of one's uniqueness.[10]

These are skills that can be learned and to that task the church must turn its attention with unprecedented urgency, for there is abundant evidence that church leaders are in urgent need.

The emergent organizational forms, that will radically affect the church along with all other institutions, constitute a shift from bureaucracy to adhocracy. The new organizational virtues will be flexibility and adaptability, with the tasks of effective institutional leadership being to "integrate . . . constellate . . . and collaborate." [11] This means new behavior; a new style of leadership by those in positions of power. My pessimistic prediction is that some will not be able to negotiate the transition into the new leadership responses required. Years of conditioning led one judicatory executive to say, "It has always worked for me in the past, why should I change now?" As with many other things in the church, we sing but fail to heed the reality of James Russell Lowell's hymn:

New occasions teach new duties,
Time makes ancient good uncouth;
They must upward still and onward,
Who would keep abreast of truth.

We can't wait. The crisis is now. Already the old bureaucratic model of leadership is subject to open ridicule and its practitioners do not command the respect or loyalty of their constituency —except as they control the ecclesiastical reward system. (In

---

[10] Bennis and Slater, op. cit., p. 128.
[11] Ibid., pp. 101, 103, 105.

politics it is called patronage.) At a recent national church gathering presided over by a heavy-handed chairman, one man turned to me at the lunch break and said, "If he (the chairman) was ever in a sensitivity group, would he get bombed." Many in the church are now experiencing more democratic leadership models that are not coercive but collaborative; that do not dictate but integrate; and encourage the open, free development of decisions rather than asking committees and groups to rubber-stamp what has already been determined in advance. The contrast in leadership styles is devastating. As painful as it will be, the ecclesiastical big daddies will either change or be discarded.

We now turn to the experience of a local parish to trace the efforts of a community of Christians seeking to put into practice new leadership styles and organizational forms.

THE UNITED PARISH OF NEWTON

Newton, Massachusetts, is a city of thirteen villages. With a population of almost 100,000—approximately 40% Jewish and 30% Catholic—the city, like many in New England, is over-supplied with Protestant churches. Built in the days of "village identity," Newton contains seven churches affiliated with the United Church of Christ. All have a long, proud history; several are handsomely endowed with trust funds; but each is suffering an increasing burden to maintain an effective, creative ministry under conditions of a shrinking support base in membership and annual financial giving. The costs of institutional maintenance cut deeper year by year into the ability of each church to carry on an effective Christian ministry.

On February 9, 1969, the ministers of the seven Newton UCC churches exchanged pulpits with one another, and that same afternoon met in one of the parsonages with two lay representatives from each congregation to discuss the future of the United Church of Christ in Newton. It was the first formal step in a process that would lead several months later to the formation of the United Parish of Newton. Circumstances dictated that the merger talks prompted four churches to seek closer ecumenical ties at the village level, leaving the First Church in Newton Centre, the Second Church in West Newton, and the Eliot Church in Newton Corner as the three UCC congregations that would seek a new relationship with one another.

Inevitably the process was slow. The three churches were

strong and vigorous, with a combined membership of almost 2,000 persons, and a solid financial base, including combined endowment assets of $750,000. Each congregation could continue to go it alone for several years. *But the handwriting was on the wall,* and there was a determination to act out of strength rather than weakness; *to choose the future for the three churches,* instead of allowing social forces to shape an unplanned future in a haphazard way.

Membership in all Protestant churches in Newton has been in sharp decline in the decades of the 50's and 60's. Figures for the three UCC churches that would form the United Parish of Newton reflect a community trend:

Church	Membership	
	1952	*1970*
Eliot	772	388
First	1,195	384
Second	1,708	1,162

From 1965 to 1970, the Second Church in West Newton sustained a net loss of 50 members each year. First Church showed a more gradual decline, while the Eliot Church remained relatively static. However, because of its particular style of ministry, the membership of the Eliot Church changed dramatically in character during this period.

Pursuing a ministry in and for the world, actively involved in issues of racism and peace, the Eliot Church increasingly drew younger, action-oriented persons into membership, while it suffered conflict and alienation among its older, long-time members. The latter group expressed its disapproval through decreased financial support, while younger members, who replaced the dissidents in leadership roles, were unable to equal their financial capabilities in supporting the institutional church. This brought the Eliot Church to a crossroads: either to link itself with other churches in the community, thereby reducing burdensome overhead costs, or to press for a more sectarian ministry with reduced institutional commitments. The heritage of a building, constructed in 1957 and valued at one million dollars, was the greatest threat to the future ministry of the Eliot Church. It was yet to be determined whether it could be an asset.

Because the members of the three churches chose to plan for

their future at a time when options were still open to them, the diverse objectives and styles of ministry inherent within the respective congregations would be vigorously defended, with an insistance that they be incorporated into any new ecclesiastical partnership. Each congregation was strong enough to choose not to enter into an organic relationship with the other two churches if their own fundamental objectives and concerns were not honored and respected by all. That fact provided the greatest source of hope that the representatives of the three churches would be forced to fashion an institutional model that would be responsive to the new leadership and organizational needs of the 70's. For the negotiators, it insured a painful process.

Throughout 1969, meetings and conversations tested the possibilities of First, Second, and Eliot Churches entering an ecclesiastical partnership. Because First Church in Newton Centre had also been carrying on informal conversations with neighboring churches of other denominations, there was the desire to explore an even more inclusive fellowship. The latter proved to be more of a hope than a real possibility, however, and in January 1970 the membership of the three congregations were asked to vote at their respective annual meetings:

> To make a commitment to seek a United Parish, working initially with the three churches represented, but open to any other churches which may wish to be represented.

Taking affirmative action on that motion, the three churches immediately appointed representatives who formed the Committee for a United Parish to negotiate the details. Again months of conversations and meetings ensued—but more intense and specific and with the help of a process consultant; and by June 1970 the committee was ready to submit to the members of the three churches a partnership plan.

June 15, 1970 was a historic moment for the First, Second, and Eliot Churches of Newton. That evening the three congregations gathered in their separate buildings to debate and vote upon the "Recommendation for a Trial Partnership." [12] The necessity for a pluralistic organizational model was clearly reflected in the preamble:

> The United Parish is committed to:

---

[12] The "Recommendation for a Trial Partnership" will be found in its entirety in the Appendix.

Encompass a diversity of approaches, methods and objectives;

Welcome people of all backgrounds;

Develop multiple forms of worship, programs, educational experience and outreach;

Be open to differing theological affirmations and forms of polity;

Promote diversified uses of its human, financial, and physical resources.

The committee also clearly recognized the tension and potential conflict within a pluralistic form and included the following statement within the Recommendation:

> In its corporate life the United Parish is dependent upon mutual trust. The voice of the individual must not be lost beneath the weight of the many; likewise, the life of the whole should not be limited by the concerted actions of the few.

Debate was long and spirited. Eliot Church was conducting a daily vigil on its lawn against the expansion of the Indochina War into Cambodia, and some members of First and Second Churches looked with some apprehension and suspicion upon affiliation with Eliot Church. In membership, the Second Church exceeded the combined totals of both First and Eliot Churches, and fear was expressed that any partnership would mean the loss of identity and style for the two smaller churches. Questions of building use, retention of staff, and budget allocations were all raised in one form or another at the three congregational meetings being held simultaneously, and then a vote was taken on the following resolution:

> That the First Church in Newton, the Second Church in Newton and Eliot Church of Newton hereby form a partnership to be known as the United Parish of Newton to carry on jointly the activities associated with the life of a church.

The moment of truth had arrived. When the ballots were counted, the members of the three congregations had all voted in the affirmative:

First Church   — 85% in favor
Second Church — 64% in favor
Eliot Church   — 70% in favor

It was an act of faith by three churches seeking to plan their future rather than drift aimlessly on the tides of inexorable change. History had come full circle. The First Church had been gathered in 1664; the Second Church was established in 1781 by members of the First Church; and in 1845, the Eliot Church was founded by those members of First Church who desired a place of worship of their own in the Newton Corner area of the city. Now the three churches, under new circumstances, were acting to renew their ties in a bold, new venture.

The working agreement of the Trial Partnership called for multiple forms of worship, educational opportunities and social action programs. The proposal affirmed:

> Institutional forms and structures must be in continuous evolution. The United Parish shall provide a framework within which existing and new groupings or clusters of people can come together to develop styles of Christian worship and mission responsive to their individual needs.

That was the vision, but its implementation continues to be a painful process. For any church the expression of the correct word has always been easy; the translation into concrete deeds has always been difficult. Using a familiar analogy: motherhood is easy to affirm, while pregnancy requires an existential act.

The tension was between *money and mission.* One seemed to stress the practical while the other lifted up the ideal, but neither issue could be isolated from the other. Understandably, many members of the three congregations saw in the partnership proposal a means to reduce substantially institutional costs and were ready to press for the elimination of one or more buildings and a reduction in the number of professional staff. But which of the three buildings should be disposed of? and which of the five staff (four ministers and one director of Christian education) should remain or go? Inevitably it was suggested that perhaps it would be best if all staff resigned if a United Parish was to be created, giving the new church the opportunity to choose its own staff unencumbered by former loyalties. For many, that argument was persuasive, but others considered it a possible "cop out." The Preamble of the partnership proposal called for diversity and pluralism. At the very outset were the three churches unable to handle the diversity and pluralism within the staff? Would the members of the three churches struggle with the issues of new styles of leadership and organizational forms? Others pressed the point that no basic decisions could be made until the mission of the United Parish was defined.

Buildings and staff were the hottest issues that confronted the congregations following the June 15 vote. Other matters also carried deep convictions and emotions, requiring adjustments in some of the proposals in the adopted partnership plan. In the months following the acceptance of the "Recommendation for a Trial Partnership" human needs, as they should, frequently superceded the more rational design of the proposal. To insure diverse forms of worship, plans were made for a traditional and contemporary service of worship each Sunday morning in the Second Church, but it was soon apparent that older members of both First and Eliot Churches needed a continuing opportunity to worship in their own buildings, at least during the first year in the life of the United Parish. The issue was not physical transportation, but emotional dislocation. The "tie that binds" is frequently attached to a building. In response, chapel services were held weekly at the First and Eliot Churches.

Other items would require a more gradual change also than recommended in the partnership plan. The suggestion to combine offices immediately would have to wait upon decisions regarding the buildings. A combined financial campaign for the three churches in the fall of 1970 anticipated one combined budget in 1971, but that had to be abandoned when the hard questions of budgetary allocation had to be made. The United Parish of Newton was caught between the scylla and charybdis of money and mission. Money raised by the combined membership fell $40,000 short of the 1970 combined budgets of the three churches. Nonetheless, there was an unwillingness to allow financial considerations alone to determine the mission of the United Parish as it related to building use, staff design and program. Therefore, each church was required to work through its own financial problems in 1971. It was a momentary reprieve in answering the hard questions, but the future was crystal clear: *unless the leadership of the churches worked imaginatively and prayerfully to make decisions based on mission, they would be overwhelmed by the necessity to make decisions based on money by 1972.* Again the issue was before us that brought the United Parish into being: could we be skillful and creative enough to plan our own future?

One of the immediate benefits of the partnership plan that would help in the determination of mission was the more flexible use of space. The Sunday morning church school program was easily absorbed within the facilities of the Second Church, making it possible for the Eliot Church to open its facilities to a community program for youth, known as *Beginnings*. It was a decision destined to illuminate, as never before, to the members of the United Parish the deep, pernicious malaise of many youth within the Newton community. For the members of the Eliot Church, *Beginnings* provided the deepest crisis within the church during my eight years of ministry. In 1964 when I went south to share in the "Mississippi Summer," I was asked by some church members, "Why must you go to Mississippi, when there is so much to do right here?" In 1967 when I was involved in Boston with anti-war protesters, who were turning in their draft cards, I was asked, "Why must you go into Boston when there is so much to do here in Newton?" In the fall of 1970, with space available in the church, the decision was made to use the facilities of the Eliot Church for a community youth program. *And never have the recriminations and trauma been greater among those members of the church who asked in 1964 and 1967 why a ministry wasn't being carried on in the neighborhood of the church.* Nothing in their church experience—which stretches over decades for many—had prepared them for their church to seek to provide a ministry to alienated youth caught in the vortex of parental rejection, academic failure, alcohol and drugs. *Beginnings*, a program of the Newton Youth Foundation, seeks to provide a community of acceptance for alienated youth in which new options of behavior can be developed other than vandalism, crime, drinking and drug use. But changes in behavior, if they develop at all, come very gradually among youth "turned off" by every social contact. By accepting *Beginnings*, the Eliot Church soon began to show ugly wounds inflicted upon a building only 12 years old. They were wounds more visible to many than those that had been deeply etched into the lives of many Newton youth. Many could not believe that these were our neighborhood youth—"they must come from somewhere else." A drug raid by state and Newton police in the spring of 1971, resulting in the arrest of more than 40 teenagers, made more visible to the community the reality that confronted the staff of *Beginnings* every day.

At issue for the members of the Eliot Church was more than damage to the building. Other programs within the church were seriously affected. When *Beginnings* opened its doors in the Eliot Church in October 1970 it was designed as an arts and crafts program that would be available five days a week within specified hours. But in the months that followed its inception, it was overwhelmed by success, numerically, and uncovered a deep need of many youth. Rejected and alienated from their homes, unwanted by merchants in their stores, and told to "move along" by the police when they congregated on street corners, many teenagers wanted a place to gather *every day of the week at all hours.* If they were not inside of the building, they would be clustered on the outside, often bringing them into hostile, angry interchanges with others who were using the Eliot Church facilities. On one occasion, one church member screamed her frustration, "You all ought to be in concentration camps."

Beginnings had opened a painful confrontation with questions relating to the mission of the church. Can a suburban church, where property values are held in high esteem and the personal prerogatives of church members are jealously guarded, provide a setting for troubled youth to meet? All congregations are familiar with the story of the Good Samaritan (Luke 10:30-37) and Jesus speaks of ministry to "the least of these my brethren (Matt. 25:40)," but so few church members have experienced this in a first-hand, personal way. The question is still before us in the United Parish of Newton, and the Eliot Church in particular, whether we can embrace the mission of *Beginnings.* But there is the conviction among some that only in the risking of its institutional life, will Christ's mission for the church be found.

The partnership plan of the United Parish also made possible experimentation in Christian education and worship, while, at the same time, preserving traditional forms. In September 1970 in conjunction with the Boston University School of Theology, a new thrust in education and worship was initiated at the Eliot Church grounded in the importance of community. Each Friday evening, families gather for dinner at 6:00 P.M.; then divide into "interest groups" at 7:00 P.M. Adult groups have centered on alternate life styles, prayer groups, theological reflections, group dynamics, issues in international development, intimacy in marriage, etc. After an hour and a half, all members of the family gather in the sanctuary for worship which is a "liturgy of the people." Different members of the community take responsibility for leadership, developing a sharing and participation which grows out of the joy and pain of the people. The variety and vitality have given many a new appreciation and experience of what it means to worship God in a community of faith. In a few months, the Friday evening experience has outstripped in attendance and participation any church program that has been held at the Eliot Church in three or four years.

The fall and winter of 1970-71 was a time of severe dislocation—both physically and psychologically—for many members of the United Parish of Newton. The Trial Partnership brought into being by affirmative action of the three churches in June 1970 raised many issues for all members. Not the least was the question whether the three churches would vote to stay together after a trial period, or would the difficult decisions that had to be made, prompt retreat and withdrawal? The proposal called for a review of the working agreement by February 15, 1972, but after a very few months it was clear that a more formal agreement and action by the congregations would be required much earlier. We could not live in a state of suspense as to whether we were going to be a united church or not. A binding decision had to be made. The organizing committee and staff agreed that a model for a United Parish would be submitted to the three congregations by February 1971. *When that decision was made, the critical issues of leadership and organizational design came into sharp focus.* Five areas held the key to the future for the First, Second and Eliot Churches of Newton:

1. Purpose: to what were we committed?
2. Programs: by whom would decisions be made?
3. Buildings: how would they be used or disposed of?
4. Staff: how would leadership and authority be distributed?
5. Budget: how would financial allocations be determined?

Many held strong convictions about these issues requiring the model builders to make carefully considered political judgments. The question was this: what had to be included to insure the continued participation of one congregation, which at the same time would be acceptable to the other two churches. Each congregation brought its own non-negotiables, and out of them the mission had to be determined and the model designed.

On February 10, 1971, members of the three churches met at the First Church to discuss a "Proposed Model for the United Parish" and then separate by congregations to vote. The statement of purpose was a reaffirmation of the Preamble in the original trial partnership. The United Parish would be committed to pluralism and diversity.

To make that commitment real, the model called for multiple

111

power centers within the United Parish allowing program initiatives to come from various sources and decentralizing the decision-making process. To maintain a creative balance between co-ordination and chaos, the proposed Standing Rules (by which the United Parish would operate until formal bylaws were accepted) created a United Parish Committee, with executive powers, *but not veto authority*. The model stated:

> The United Parish Committee shall be responsible for co-ordination and constructive evaluation of all activities. If and when conflicts arise, there will be congregational control administered through the United Parish Committee, or a congregational meeting.

Conflicts and differences that could not be adjudicated by the United Parish Committee would be submitted to congregational authority in keeping with the traditional polity of the three churches. The organizational design of the model insured no one line of authority or locus of power. The design places a premium on political skills in an open, self-conscious way. In most churches political power is frequently hidden beneath layers of piety. All organizations construct their own power model overtly or covertly. The model of the United Parish of Newton chose to make the power issue manifest to all that it might be dealt with openly and constructively.

The issue of buildings was caught between personal attachments, financial costs and the needs for an adequate real estate base to insure pluralism and diversity. No member wanted to give up his building, but some adjustments would be required, for the institutional costs of maintaining three buildings were prohibitive and poor stewardship of resources. The model called for the retention of two buildings with the stipulation that Second Church, which had invested $200,000 in its building in 1968-69, would be one of the two. The proposal rejected a one-building model as an inadequate base for pluriform ministries, at least in the immediate future.

Staff design and the locus of authority was one of the most sensitive areas of the model. The tenure of the five professional staff ranged from a few months to sixteen years. Loyalties had been established and constituencies were jealous to protect their minister. It gave force to the recommendation of some, that all staff should resign, allowing a newly formed United Parish to choose its own leadership.

But other considerations prevailed for the moment. More was

at stake than tenure and identity. If pluralism and diversity were to be the life-style of the United Parish, the staff should represent the polarizations and differences even at the cost of conflict and pain. Tension that kept the issues alive was more important than harmony that yielded complacency.

A leadership design suitable for the new organizational developments of the 70's and 80's was a priority. Bureaucracy, which has been the prevailing organizational model of the church, anticipates a hierarchial leadership design. Within bureaucracy there is the need to identify who is in charge. But adhocracy, grounded in an organizational structure calling for multiple power centers, makes possible a team ministry. With that need in mind, the proposed model for the United Parish recommended "co-ministers with clearly defined areas of responsibility." In addition the proposed staff design stated:

> A ministerial relations committee of six (6) lay members, two from each church and one of whom shall be a deacon, shall work closely with the staff to co-ordinate the abilities and interests of the staff with the needs of the parish.

The recommendation envisioned a leadership style that would be new and untested for both the members of the congregations and the staff.

Some insights into the critical issues to be "worked through" by the proposed team ministry are lifted up in a Team Development Scale devised by management consultants, Douglas McGregor and John Paul Jones. Warren Bennis reproduces the crude scale in his book on *Organizational Development*:

Team Development Scale [13]

1. Degree of mutual trust:
   High suspicion ——————————High trust
      (1)   (4)   (7)

2. Communications:
   Guarded, cautious ——————————Open, authentic
      (1)   (4)   (7)

3. Degree of mutual support: Genuine concern for
   Every man for himself ——————————each other
      (1)   (4)   (7)

4. Team objectives:
   Not understood ——————————Clearly understood
      (1)   (4)   (7)

---

[13] Bennis, op. cit., p. 3.

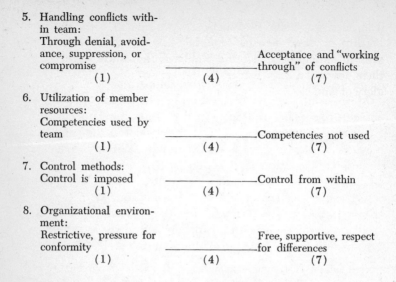

5. Handling conflicts within team:
   Through denial, avoidance, suppression, or compromise
   (1)   (4)   Acceptance and "working through" of conflicts
   (7)

6. Utilization of member resources:
   Competencies used by team
   (1)   (4)   Competencies not used
   (7)

7. Control methods:
   Control is imposed
   (1)   (4)   Control from within
   (7)

8. Organizational environment:
   Restrictive, pressure for conformity
   (1)   (4)   Free, supportive, respect for differences
   (7)

The model presented a leadership design that was a challenge in cooperation for the staff and would test their maturity to the utmost. It would mean learning new skills and putting them into practice in the local church.

In the area of finances, the model anticipated deficit spending and the use of endowment principle into 1972. Reduction in institutional expenditures was essential, but if that need could be combined with a clear vision of mission and purpose, in combination with a leadership and organizational design commensurate with the needs of today, then there was reason for hope that the United Parish could plan for its future intelligently and creatively. On that hope rested the "Proposed Model for the United Parish" submitted to the congregations of First, Second, and Eliot Churches on February 10, 1971.

Discussion and debate was more intense than the preceding June. There was consensus that an affirmative vote on the model would end the trial partnership and establish the foundation for a merger among the three churches. With feelings of uncertainty and anticipation, the votes were cast, yielding the following results:

First Church   — 74% in favor
Second Church — 63% in favor
Eliot Church   — 75% in favor

The deed was done. In a mood of anxiety and hope, the membership of three Newton churches had set their ecclesiastical sails in anticipation that the winds of the Spirit might propel them toward a new future in the service of man and to the glory of God.

Chapter 5
TEMPLE AND TENT-MAKING MINISTRIES

> The woman said to him. . . . "Our fathers worshiped on this mountain; and you say that in Jerusalem is the place where men ought to worship." Jesus said to her, "Woman, believe me, the hour is coming when neither on this mountain nor in Jerusalem will you worship the Father." . . . The true worshipers will worship the Father in spirit and in truth.
>
> John 4:19-21, 23

If there is one lesson the years of Christian ministry have taught me it is this: the life and death issues for the church will only come alive in the hot matrix of decision-making. To that conviction I would add another: the rhetoric of Christian faith will become reality only when the believing Christian tests his convictions through costly choices. To play it safe is to insure death. To make decisions that risk the life of the institutional church and one's own security is to hover between the possibilities of life and death—with the ultimate disposition in the hands of God. One can never be certain in advance, and he who wants a sign only demonstrates his own unbelief. This is God's world, and each is called, in the words of Paul, to "work out your own salvation with fear and trembling; for God is at work in you (Phil. 2:12-13)."

The Consultation on Church Union (COCU) is occupying much attention among some church leaders today. It could prove to be of great significance, or it could be an escape from the hard decisions confronting the church. The danger is that it will produce an ecclesiastical design that, on paper, lumps millions of Christians under one church structure but is irrelevant in developing the church's capacity for ministry in a radically changing society. We are witnessing the collapse of all institutions—ecclesiastical, educational and political. What is needed for the future has not yet been designed. Councils of churches —local, national and international—as they have existed in the past, appear increasingly unrelated to the person in the pulpit and the pew and too timorous to respond effectively to the world's agenda. The new forms of organizational structures and new styles of leadership needed will be as difficult to put into practice among churches of the same denomination as across denominational lines. The irony is that COCU could achieve success that would have had significance at the turn of the twentieth century, but is hopelessly irrelevant to meet the systemic changes now required in the church. No rearrangement of the old is adequate; we need the emergence of the new, despite the pain and dislocation that will bring.

When the Mission Priorities Council met in February 1971, the executive director characterized the United Church of Christ as "50 satrapies," each vying to maintain its own ecclesiastical kingdom.[1] His words offended some present and a motion was made to strike his definition of the church from the record. The urgent need is for the church to look honestly and painfully at itself. It is hard to be honest and open, but it will become increasingly more difficult for the church if it deceives itself and is defensive. Vulnerability is a way to freedom both for the individual and the institution.

United Churchmen for Change—a reform group within the United Church of Christ—includes clergy and lay men and women who care deeply and passionately for the church of Christ, and, out of their concern, adopted the following statement of purpose:

> United Churchmen for Change recognize that the Christian Church exists in the midst of a world-wide revolution spurred by the efforts of the dispossessed to claim their full human rights.
>
> We support this surge for freedom and new life as evidence of God at work in our midst and a new opportunity to deliver the powerful from their bondage to wealth and privilege.
>
> We are committed to the power struggle required to bring change. As a first step, we call upon all agencies of the United Church of Christ to declare their priorities and commitments in the use of their property, financial resources, and personnel.
>
> While working within the United Church of Christ, we shall press for required structural changes. We seek election to positions of power representative of all segments of the church. We solicit cooperation with groups similar to our own in other denominations.[2]

How is the church to be alive? allowing the Spirit to revitalize the "dry bones." How is the church to be response-able to the challenges and demands of the new day? Whether it is COCU,

---

[1] Mineo Katagari, Cleveland, Ohio, February 3, 1971. The 50 satrapies refer to the 40 conferences and 10 instrumentalities.

[2] Adopted by the Executive Committee of United Churchmen for Change, September 1969

the Mission Priorities Council, a state conference, United Churchmen for Change or any other ecclesiastical agency or group; the challenge is for leadership that has a vision for the seventies and eighties, persons able to risk the organizational changes required, and men and women willing to calculate the cost and still forge ahead with faith and hope and joy. "Which of you desiring to build a tower, does not first sit down and count the cost, whether he has enough to complete it (Luke 14:28)?" And there is a price, as with everything else that is worthwhile.

When Robert V. Moss, Jr., president of the United Church of Christ, issued an invitation to all conference ministers and presidents to join him in the Moratorium against the Vietnam War in Washington, D. C., November 1969, one conference sent a letter to its constituent churches telling of the invitation and suggesting that the conference might arrange a bus to transport church members to the nation's capital. Later the Conference Minister told me that in two instances that letter cost the conference at least $12,000 in contributions that year. There is an "in house" saying among conference leaders when a stand is taken on peace, race or poverty—"There goes a few more OCWM (Our Christian World Mission) bucks." It is tragic indeed, that many find it more difficult in the church to take moral stands on critical issues than in secular organizations.

The Christian imperative is to break out of the safety of our sanctuaries and risk our institutional lives and personal security in the world where God's children cry out in need. We remember the words, "Come, O blessed of my Father. . . . Depart from me, you cursed (Matt. 25:34, 41)." On taking up the world's agenda, Congressman Robert F. Drinan of the Third Congressional District in Massachusetts had this to say:

> Christians in America have . . . assumed that the government of the United States will in general follow those moral norms that most Christian denominations in America would accept. I submit that the time has come to re-examine this assumption. . . . When a government continues to wage a brutal and genocidal war contrary to the statements of virtually all of the churches of America one must very bluntly raise the question whether this government is in fact guided by any of the great moral traditions. . . .
> The churches in America have customarily isolated themselves from political power. The assumption has been that the churches could by their teachings educate a sufficient number of well-informed and devout Christians who would carry into public life those

moral and spiritual norms which are common to all religions in America and which form the moral consensus on which American democracy was founded. In view, however, of the ghastly problems of war, white racism and persistent poverty in America it would appear that the time has come for the churches to re-examine their traditional policy of assuming that an adequate number of morally sophisticated persons would emerge from the churches . . .[3]

In a new way the Christian church is forced to ask whether the cross or the American flag is the *central* symbol of faith?

I remember the service of worship on October 15, 1967, at the Arlington Street Church, Boston. Over 250 young men turned in their draft cards to clergy or burned them at the altar of the church.[4] After that act, bread was passed as a symbol of man's life and unity. For many it was the bread of communion. Tears streamed down the faces of some, for it was not a perfunctory ritual, it was breaking and sharing a loaf *after a costly act of dedication.* Those who relinquished their draft cards were subject to imprisonment. One would not want to vouch for the motivations of all, but that a costly religious commitment had been made specific by some was apparent. In conversations with my fellow clergymen we compared that service with the sacrament of communion that is offered regularly in such a casual way, unrelated to costly discipleship, and we knew why the church is often found to be impotent and irrelevant to life's critical issues.

Some years earlier, July 1964 to be exact, in the Sun and Sands Motel, Jackson, Mississippi, I sat on the bed and read the 12th chapter of Romans to a former deacon of the Eliot Church. The words literally leapt out of the pages at us for we had just returned from Greenwood, Mississippi, where we had participated in a voter registration drive that led to more than 100 persons being arrested. Scripture took on a fresh new meaning as I read the words:

> I appeal to you therefore, brethren, by the mercies of God, to present your bodies as a living sacrifice, holy and acceptable to God, which is your spiritual worship.
> Romans 12:1

---

[3] An address before the Annual Meeting of the Massachusetts Conference of the United Church of Christ, May 7, 1971, quoted by permission of the author.

[4] It was their participation in this service that led to the indictment of the Rev. William Sloan Coffin, Jr., and Michael Ferber, both among the "Boston Five."

We had seen young men and women place their bodies on the line in behalf of God's children.

Another writer of scripture expressed it so well, when he referred to Jesus, "who for the joy that was set before him endured the cross (Heb. 12:2)." Christian ministry, as I know it, is a mixture of pain and joy—not always in that order and seldom in balanced quantities. I am convinced that God is at work in our midst. It is a time of great wrenching, but also a moment of exploding possibilities. The wall between hope and despair is thin. I opt for hope and ask help from those around me in my times of despair. I choose to try to live and minister as if this were the first day of the rest of my life.

APPENDIX

RECOMMENDATION FOR A TRIAL PARTNERSHIP
(United Parish of Newton)

PREAMBLE

God calls His Church into being to effect His will in the world. We, the members of The First Church in Newton, The Second Church in Newton, and Eliot Church of Newton seek to respond to this charge by forming a United Parish which will:

Provide maximum support for the various Christian witnesses of its members;

Minister to its members as their individual needs manifest;

Facilitate development of intimate groupings of members who can minister to each other and to society's needs;

Testify to the ability of the Christian, acting in love, to gain strength through interaction with others.

Thus, the United Parish is committed to:

Encompass a diversity of approaches, methods and objectives;

Welcome people of all backgrounds;

Develop multiple forms of worship, programs, educational experience and outreach;

Be open to differing theological affirmations and forms of polity;

Promote diversified uses of its human, financial, and physical resources.

In its corporate life the United Parish is dependent upon mutual trust. The voice of the individual must not be lost beneath the weight of the many; likewise, the life of the whole should not be limited by the concerted actions of the few.

The United Parish, with its resources imaginatively employed, can:

Provide specialized ministries by its multiple staff;

123

Utilize the rich reservoir of talents possessed by its members;

Employ its material assets effectively on behalf of the church's mission;

Devise and undertake services not presently available in the individual churches;

Speak with love and power on issues of concern.

RESOLUTION

That the First Church in Newton, the Second Church in Newton and Eliot Church of Newton hereby form a partnership to be known as The United Parish of Newton to carry on jointly the activities associated with the life of a church. *Until later replaced by more formal by-laws, the following trial Partnership Proposal shall be our working agreement.*

PARTNERSHIP PROPOSAL

I. The Partnership

The United Parish shall be a partnership with the three churches named above as the original partners. The partnership, however, is open at any time to other churches of any denomination which may wish to join. In addition, the United Parish shall be open to cooperative action in any areas of concern with other churches or groups of churches.

A. Membership

Membership in the United Parish will be automatic for members of First, Second and Eliot Churches, and be open to others who affirm its principles.

B. Legal Existence

Legal existence of each church will be maintained for the purpose of holding title to assets. Each of the three original member churches shall retain its membership in the United Church of Christ.

II. Ministries
A. Worship

Beginning in September of 1970, there shall be initially two worship services, one traditional and another contemporary, on Sundays at Second Church. Other worship opportunities will be provided as called for.

B. Christian Education

Beginning in September of 1970, Christian Education will be provided on Sundays at the place of worship. Additional opportunities will be offered for families, youth and adults at various times and locations.

C. Outreach

The Social Action, Benevolence, and Outreach Committees of the three churches will continue together to plan and implement the work of Christian Outreach for the United Parish.

D. Clusters

Institutional forms and structures must be in continuous evolution. The United Parish shall provide a framework within which existing and new groupings or clusters of people can come together to develop styles of Christian worship and mission responsive to their individual needs.

III. Standing Committees

The comparable standing committees of the three churches, working together, shall be responsible for planning and carrying out activities in the areas delegated to them until such time as committees are elected for the United Parish. Insofar as possible, there shall be equal representation from each member church on all standing committees.

IV. Staff

It is hoped that staff members will continue with the United Parish. Functions of the staff will be determined by the professional leadership and a personnel committee of three, one to be appointed by each church.

V. Buildings

At the outset, all buildings will be retained. The type of continued use or the disposition of buildings will be determined by a survey of all factors, in the light of actual experience, needs, and opportunities for alternate use. No one of the member churches will dispose of its properties without the concurrence of the other members of the United Parish partnership.

A. Effective September 1970, although some activities such as the nursery school will continue at First Church, its sanctuary will be closed.

B. When not being used for an activity of the United Parish, space in any of the United Parish properties is available for community use and for housing new ministries.

VI. Offices

All the professional staff of the United Parish will, if possible, have offices in a single church. Eliot Church is presently believed the best location.

VII. Finances

A. Each church shall complete its 1970 budgets by separation of collections and expenses for the balance of 1970.

B. As of January, 1971, there shall be one financial operation, with one joint United Parish Budget and one joint Outreach Budget developed and supervised by the designated joint committees.

C. After January 1, 1971, undesignated endowment fund income received by each church shall be turned over to the joint budget. Where special purposes were designated, such income shall be so used.

D. Endowment fund assets are to remain in the legal title of each church but shall be subject to cooperative investment management.

E. A single fund-raising campaign shall be carried out in the fall of 1970 by the cooperative efforts of present Finance and Outreach Committees.

VIII. Organizing

A. An organizing committee shall be appointed immediately, consisting of three members from each of the partner churches, with the ministerial staff. This committee shall have the authority to carry out the intent of this resolution, may appoint committees to deal with specific problems as required, and will constitute an executive committee for the United Parish until officers and committees are elected at a United Parish Annual Meeting to be held not later than February 15,

1971. In the interim, this organizing committee will make reports to the appropriate Governing or Administrative Boards of the three churches.

B. By-laws for the United Parish shall be proposed by a committee consisting of two members selected by each church which shall report by January, 1971, in time for the United Parish Annual Meeting. Each individual church will also have its own by-laws.

C. This working agreement shall be reviewed by the respective churches no later than February 15, 1972.

D. The United Parish shall become effective when this resolution is adopted by all three initial church partners.

Approved by the Committee for a United Parish
May 19, 1970